AI for the Curious Worker:

An Eye Opener to the Prospects of Automated Labor.

AI for the Curious Worker

Copyright 2023, Micheal Lee

Introduction

Artificial intelligence (AI) is transforming the world of work in unprecedented ways. From self-driving cars to chatbots, AI is creating new opportunities and challenges for workers across various sectors and industries. How can we prepare for the future of work in the age of AI? What are the skills and competencies that will be in high demand in the coming years? How can we leverage AI to enhance our creativity, productivity and well-being? These are some of the questions that this book aims to answer. In this book, you will discover the emerging jobs that are powered by AI, such as data analysts, machine learning engineers, content creators and more. You will also learn about the skills and mindsets that are essential for succeeding in these jobs, such as critical thinking, collaboration, curiosity and adaptability. Whether you are a student, a professional, an entrepreneur or a lifelong learner, this book will help you navigate the changing landscape of work and thrive in the era of AI. This could also serve as an educational copy for the upbringing of the younger generation of workers and preparation them for an automated workplace.

Contents

Part One: The New Guy Called AI

AI and the Shocking Rumors

You would remember that since the beginning of the 20th century, people have nursed the idea that a day would come that robots would take over the world. This was due to the high rate of innovation and emergence of many technologies that could do everything better than humans. However, the thought only occurred as an idea back then. Many people today, and that includes me, you and most of the guys you work with are starting to feel the reality of this prophesy. I have a cousin, Martin. He is a personal assistant to the CEO at a socks manufacturing company and he used to complain of his boss, Jonathan. He always says Jonathan could do nothing by himself and always dumps everything on him. You know the typical boss type who gets lazy once they get an employee. And Martin would come home all shrewd up and tired. We used to stay in the same apartment and I always felt do much pity for him. He was very fat but since he started work at the company, his mother kept complaining of his sunken eyes and even if I didn't notice that, I couldn't have missed his pot belly which became fat after three months of working for Mr. Jonathan or Jonadamn as he always says. He would slam the door and yell "How can a CEO not write his own mails?" and then fling the shirt at me. "Does he have to suck at writing just because he is good at making sucks?" The next thing he did was grab a bear and sink into the sofa like sick puppy.

But recently, I discovered some changes. This 30 years old cry baby suddenly stopped crying about his work and started coming home early with smiles, his tie knotted and his sleeves unfolded. But also he had stopped bringing home groceries he bought from the tips he used to get Jonathan.

I didn't say anything. I just sat at my computer and did my thing. And he would come and tap me on the shoulder and say "Good boy, well done. I wish you enjoy the fun of office work before you age out of your mobile devices". And one day he yelled, "get up and have some exposure you cyber addict!" And I was the joke for the time his boss wasn't frustrating him with overwork and overtime. And then, one Sunday afternoon while watching TV together, a notification popped on his phone and I could instantly read the despair on his face.

"What's up bro?" I asked.

He looked up lifted brows and a drawn up forehead. That's not a good sign. I was able to peep and I saw that it was his paycheck.

"I have been short paid again" He said in a low and defeated tone.

"But why? Maybe call the accountant"

"No, it's not him; it's Jonadamn, that asshole!"

Later in the day, while we played a video game, he confessed to me that he has been receiving only half of his weekly pay for the past three weeks. Well, I wasn't shocked. I have been paying most of the bills we shared and I was going to make him pay alone for the following weeks. And I didn't ask because I usually never had to ask. But as it was, and since I am the older one, I had to continue. I sat him down and asked him if he was shocked when it started happening.

"Of course I was, I mean, why would he short-pay me like that without prior information. I asked the accountant in the first week and all that freak said was "speak to the boss" and I was like reaaally! Who the hell does that?"

"And have you spoken to Jonathan?" I asked

"Yes, he said he is making some adjustments and things would improve.... I don't understand how cutting my salary is an improvement". He said angrily almost yelling.

"But you were not this angry when you started coming home earlier and doing less overtime and overwork, were you?" I knew he would not understand what I meant and might mistake it for a mockery. He has a quite naïve and simple mindset and doesn't look deeper into things. Maybe that's why he just trusted his boss when he was told his salary cut was a step to some improvements. And he actually didn't understand. He turned to me with a confused glare so I had to break it down.

"You should have asked questions when your role and work were being reduced Martin, the moment you started doing less work, you should have seen that it implied less pay. Let us take it simply and logical. The lesser you do, the lesser you earn. That's the basic theorem of working. You had roles and now you no longer have them just as you had tips and now you longer have them. The same goes for your salary. Jonathan probably now has someone else or something else playing those roles he stopped calling you for and it won't be long before that thing or that person takes your place completely" I was frank and serious in my tone. Yeah. I was actually being the older brother here. It's the call I have to take from time to time and I got quite used to it.

He fixed a stern glare at me as I talked. We had both paused the game and then resting our backs on the sofa. He took some lone time thinking about what I said and he made up his mind to talk to his boss about it in a meeting. What I saw on his face was a different feeling. Not the feeling of anger for the pay-cut but a fear for the coming months. He had realized the truth that less work sometimes might mean more fun but it can also mean fewer funds. He was afraid of losing any more roles and getting a lower pay.

Now, losing roles is really close to losing jobs. In-fact, losing roles is the beginning of losing jobs which implies losing pay and going broke. Securing your job in the era of automation with AI is a serious issue no one should ignore. It may not affect everyone but it sure affects a lot of people and it only takes time for the bots to evolve and spread their touch across industries. And while it may not threaten your job, it may threaten the kind of service you receive. So, one way or the other, you are one of us: the people slightly or really threatened by AI. Let's dive into the reality.

Truly having a job should come with the assurance that you will keep the job without the risk of becoming unemployed. In the era of automation and Artificial Intelligence, job security is becoming more important than ever, as many workers face the threat of being replaced by machines or algorithms designed with artificial intelligence. Artificial Intelligence refers to the ability of machines or software to perform tasks that typically require human intelligence, such as visual perception, speech recognition, decision-making, and problem-solving. AI can be divided into two categories: narrow or weak AI, which is designed to perform specific tasks, and general or strong AI, which has the ability to perform any intellectual task that a human can do. Narrow AI is used in many applications today, such as voice assistants, image recognition, and recommendation systems. Strong AI, on the other hand, is still in the realm of theoretical research and development. Truly, these are beautiful innovations which have improved workplaces and how people work over the past decades. I am sure that if Martin had snuck up on Jonathan, he would have caught the new team mate on his computer or on his phone.

Chapter One: AI in the Workplace

It is fun to have a new female team member who makes everything easier and faster. However, when that team member has the ability to do everything you do better than you, she is no longer your team member. She becomes a threat to your job. But first, the first thing you notice about the new sexy team member is her beauty and beautiful sense of fashion. The potentials of AI can never be overemphasized as it has been proven to be impressively effective and efficient in perform many tasks across many niches, fields and industry. AI is changing the way we work and live. They are creating new opportunities for businesses, society, and individuals. Let's look at the features of AI as one brilliant, intelligent, resourceful and sexy team mate who has been wowing the entire team at the workplace since she joined.

Superfast

One of the beauties of AI as a member of your team is that it eases work by reducing time and energy spent on workloads by other team members. That AI guy is super-fast as in, super-fast. While it takes you, a PhD holder spend hours to come up with solutions to problems, AI has it in the hands of your employer in minutes. And yes, do you want to check how accurate and verifiable that data is or how well the job is done? don't even bother. It's foolproof. One day, Martin came home and was like "Oh, Jonadamn is an asshole."

"Why would you say that?" I asked, wondering what could have crossed them again since he recently told me that his pay was improved without him getting additional roles. That was after someone called Jonathan and talked to him about the Fair Labor Standards Act.

"Well, he made me enter a competition with him only down me down for a hundred bucks. He is so cheap and I know he cheated with that AI thing"

"What did he ask you to do?" I asked almost bursting from how much I tried to suppress the laughter that was swelling in me with the way Martin looked like someone who had been robbed of his last card.

"We entered some writing competition, first to send 2000 words of the best marketing ideas to the marketing department wins"

"And he won right?"

"He couldn't have pulled that off. normally, he literally takes hours to write a simple letter. And his mail got better ratings than mine. He just kept looking for ways to show me that he doesn't need me in that office. I hope he enjoys the office all by himself when he finally decides. One minute, he says I should do something, the next minute he says I shouldn't bother that he has already done it. It's really frustrating".

"There is a bright side to it," I said. "It seems your job is about to be taken by an AI? At least now you will finally have time to catch up on all the Netflix shows you've been missing."

Well, I am so sure that there is at least one million people whose boss is stressing over because of some really awesome software they just downloaded. Speed, like punctuality is the soul of business getting things done at the right time is as important as getting things done at all. And AI is the new guy that's probably showing your boss that he could do a lot of things faster even without you. To an extent, if you allow it, depending on your type of job, this new guy might leave you with nothing else to do other than prompting it. Believe me, AI is increasingly becoming an essential tool for time-saving in today's flash-like world we are now living in. It is capable of analyzing vast amounts of data quickly, identifying patterns, and making predictions, all of which can save time for businesses and individuals alike. AI-powered tools and applications can automate routine tasks, enabling employees to focus on more complex and creative work that requires their expertise. One of the key ways AI saves time is through automation. AI-powered tools can automate a variety of tasks, such as data entry, scheduling appointments, and generating reports. These tasks can be completed much faster and with greater accuracy than if done manually, saving employees valuable time that can be redirected towards more critical tasks. For instance, in healthcare, AI can help physicians by automating time-consuming tasks like patient data analysis, freeing up their time to focus on treatment planning and patient care

A lot of people have entered competition with AI and have failed. If we compare a supercomputer running a sophisticated deep learning algorithm with a human brain, then the AI would have an edge in speed and accuracy for many tasks, such as recognizing faces, searching for names, doing research and translating languages. AI can also save time by providing employees with real-time insights and recommendations. With AI-powered analytics, businesses can quickly identify trends and patterns in data, enabling them to make better and faster decisions. For example, AI-powered chatbots can help businesses respond to customer queries instantly, saving employees valuable time. Similarly, in manufacturing, AI can help identify production inefficiencies and optimize production schedules, reducing costs and saving time.

Another way AI saves time is by reducing errors and increasing accuracy. "Oh, when are you gonna be done?" Your boss would yell. And there is you doing the analysis over and over again. Whereas, AI-powered tools are capable of analyzing vast amounts of data quickly, identifying patterns, and making predictions. This not only saves time but also improves accuracy, reducing the risk of errors and improving overall productivity. For example, AI-powered financial analysis tools can quickly and accurately analyze financial data, providing insights that can help businesses make better investment decisions.

Basically, AI is a valuable time-saving tool for businesses and individuals alike. By automating routine tasks, providing real-time insights, and increasing accuracy, AI can help businesses become more efficient, productive, and profitable. And it's really hard to beat when it comes to speed and accuracy.

Crazy Efficiency

Well, no matter how much you try, your boss still complains right? "Oh, you should have done this and that, bla bla bla." Well, newsflash, your boss is about to get a new employee that'll tire them with efficiency. Someone tried to make a joke about AI and said "I thought I had a great sense of direction until I followed an AI's GPS instructions and ended up in a cornfield. At least the corn was tasty." You probably prompted the AI to take you to the place you need most to be and it took your hungry self to replenish. You are welcome.

According to most users and researcher, with the right prompts, AI tools and algorithms can perform the most complex tasks efficiently with 100% accuracy. Yeah,, just like your car. It's as good as you drive it. AI has the potential to greatly contribute awesome efficiency in a wide range of industries and applications. One of the ways AI ensures and achieves efficiency is by automating repetitive and time-consuming tasks. For example, in manufacturing, AI-powered robots shove the big guys aside and handle tasks such as assembly line work or quality control inspections, freeing up fleshy workers to focus on more creative tasks in which they are now even beginning to rely on the ghost counterparts of the robots. Similarly, in customer service, AI-powered chatbots now handle large volume of inquiries without the need for human intervention, allowing customer service teams to focus on more complex and high-value interactions, like lobbying and blackmailing investors.

Another way this new hot employee beats regular efficiency is that it has the ability to provide data-driven insights and analysis. AI algorithms can analyze large amounts of data quickly and accurately, identifying patterns and insights that would be difficult for humans to detect. This can be particularly useful in industries such as finance and healthcare, where data analysis is a critical part of decision-making processes. By providing data-driven insights, AI helps the employers and bosses make more informed decisions and improve operational efficiency. That is probably why they no longer call all those long boring meetings in which the only thing interesting is the drunk you can see from the window trying to cross the road.

AI can also improve efficiency by improving decision-making processes. By analyzing data and providing insights, AI can help decision-makers make more informed and accurate decisions. Sarah was convinced she could outsmart the AI that had been brought in to help with her job as a financial analyst. She worked late into the night, pouring over spreadsheets and crunching numbers until her eyes crossed. But when she presented her findings to her boss the next day, the AI's analysis was not only faster, but more accurate. Sarah was promptly replaced by the robot, and decided to take up a new hobby: crocheting hats for her cat. Clearly in finance, AI algorithms have proven to have the impressive ability to analyze market data and make investment recommendations, while in healthcare, AI-powered diagnostic tools can help doctors make more accurate diagnoses. By improving decision-making processes, AI can help organizations save time and resources, and achieve better outcomes and I guess Sarah's boss knew just that.

"I'm pretty sure the only thing you are better at than the AI that's replacing you is taking long lunches and pretending to be busy." I said to my cousin, Martin and he burst into a huge guffy laughter. Yeah, I got him.

Generally, AI has the potential to greatly improve efficiency across a wide range of industries and applications. By automating repetitive tasks, providing data-driven insights, and improving decision-making processes, AI can help organizations save time and resources, and achieve better outcomes.

Maximum Productivity

Oh, so there you are, wondering what's the point? Well, speed and competency makes the nucleus of productivity. And believe me; we have all been slacking off. We are all getting old and we no longer have that vigor in us like we did when we just started the job. And what does the employer really want, not diminishing return but increased productivity. And this is how the employers think of AI, a highly productive worker in many ways! AI systems are designed to perform tasks that would otherwise require human intelligence, such as analyzing large data sets, recognizing patterns, making predictions, and even engaging in complex decision-making processes. And guess what, these things work wonders.

Like imagine that superfast fast and efficient worker who has the ability to work tirelessly and without breaks or distractions. Unlike Martin and that co-worker of his who work for two hours and take a break for three, AI can work continuously without the need to rest or take a break. These systems of living and ghost robots can process vast amounts of data and cover so much workload at a speed that far exceeds what any human could achieve. This means that AI can perform repetitive, time-consuming tasks at a fraction of the time it would take a human to complete them.

Additionally, AI systems are highly adaptable and can be trained to perform a wide range of tasks across various industries. For example, in manufacturing, AI-powered robots can be used to assemble products with greater efficiency and precision than human workers. In healthcare, AI systems can be used to analyze medical images and help doctors make more accurate diagnoses.

AI can also help ensure maximum productivity by improving the accuracy and speed of decision-making processes. By analyzing data and providing insights, AI can help decision-makers make more informed and accurate decisions in less time. For example, in finance, AI algorithms can analyze market data and make investment recommendations more quickly and accurately than human analysts. In healthcare, AI-powered diagnostic tools can help doctors make more accurate diagnoses more quickly, leading to better patient outcomes.

Summarily, when you think of why the employers are on the side of the side of the robots, believe me, it's nothing personal. They understand that AI can ensure maximum productivity and the bonus, they don't have to pay extra for extra time.

Great with Customers

Okay, I know the customers like to see your face, but can you also effectively provide answers to all their questions? And, you would most likely get frustrated when the questions become a ton. And then you get tired of sitting all day waiting for frustrated people to add their frustration to yours. Well, there comes this guy called AI whom the employees can be a better customer service agent in many ways. One of the biggest advantages of putting AI in customer service is its ability to provide 24/7 support to customers without any downtime. This means that customers can get the help they need at any time, regardless of whether it's during business hours or when workers are already inn their homes having a good meal or a good sleep.

Another reason why your boss probably prefers the robot to handle customer service is that it can handle a large volume of inquiries simultaneously, without getting overwhelmed or losing track of any requests. AI chatbots, for example, can interact with multiple customers at the same time and provide quick, personalized responses to their queries. Like, this guy won't literally get lost or forget orders and queries just because two customers are asking at the same time. And you will be like "what did you say again?"

AI can also provide consistent and accurate responses to customer inquiries, as it is trained to follow predefined rules and processes. This ensures that customers receive accurate information and solutions to their problems every time, without any human error.

Moreover, AI can also help to reduce customer wait times by providing immediate assistance and solutions to common issues. This can result in a better overall customer experience, as customers are more likely to be satisfied when their issues are resolved quickly and they don't have to wait until someone finishes in the restroom.

AI can also personalize the customer experience by analyzing customer data and providing personalized recommendations and solutions. For example, AI algorithms can analyze a customer's purchase history and browsing behavior to provide personalized product recommendations. This can help businesses build stronger relationships with their customers by providing a more personalized and relevant experience.

Finally, AI can improve customer experience by providing a seamless and consistent experience across multiple channels. With AI-powered tools, businesses can provide a consistent experience across channels such as social media, email, and chat. This can help businesses build stronger relationships with their customers by providing a seamless and integrated experience.

Error Free

To err is human, right? We all make mistakes and it's normal. But then, sometimes our mistakes and errors become consistent due to certain situations that are beyond our control. Like spilling coffee over the keyboard. But your boss already knows it's in the spirit of the battle against AI. And more than that, some people just feel like, "Oh, my boss has been an asshole, he yells at me at every opportunity he gets. Maybe I should just remove a bolt in his motorcycle. A sprained ankle won't hurt too much."

Every boss want an employee they can trust 100% not to ruin their work or life no matter how much they bully them. That is why they are all rooting for the robots that have no feeling of embarrassment or revenge. They know that AI can be a worker that doesn't commit errors, or at least significantly reduces the likelihood of errors compared to you and me. They are aware of the great ability of these ghosts to perform tasks with a high level of accuracy and consistency, which can greatly reduce the risk of errors and mistakes.

Unlike my cousin Martin, AI systems don't get tired, distracted, or make mistakes due to emotions or biases. AI systems can process large amounts of data quickly and accurately, and make decisions based on objective criteria and rules that are programmed into them. This means that AI systems can perform tasks with a much higher level of precision and accuracy than human workers.

Moreover, AI systems can continuously learn and improve over time, reducing the likelihood of errors and improving their performance. They can analyze data, identify patterns and trends, and adjust their algorithms to improve their accuracy and effectiveness. This means that as an AI system works, it becomes increasingly efficient and effective, further reducing the risk of errors.

AI has the potential to make work error-free by automating tasks that are prone to human error. For example, in manufacturing, AI-powered robots can handle tasks such as assembly line work or quality control inspections with a high level of accuracy and consistency, reducing the likelihood of errors. Similarly, in finance, AI algorithms can analyze market data and make investment recommendations without the emotional biases that can lead to errors in human decision-making.

Another way AI can make work error-free is by providing real-time feedback and error detection. With AI-powered tools, businesses can quickly identify errors and inconsistencies in their data, allowing them to quickly address issues before they become major problems. This can be particularly useful in industries such as healthcare, where errors can have serious consequences for patient safety.

So, we are all prepared for the welcome party even though we have our doubts. AI has come to stay and many workers are about to get hit with realities beyond their imagination. She's hot, sexy, tall, slender, beautiful, brilliant and smart and with the way she keeps going in and out of the boss's office, she would soon become the favorite employee. What's that smirk on you face, you have won the employee of the year for years. Don't be selfish. Get over her, we have a welcome party to plan.

Chapter Two: The Welcome Party

You can imagine this party everyone is invited to but they don't want to come. But because it was the boss who asked, we all drag our sad faces to the show. Well, here we are to celebrate and welcome the one person who has the ability to do all our jobs altogether. And what's the dress code again? Fear! Everyone had it on their faces but not at first but from the moment they all learnt that the boss had invested so much money to bring in an AI system into the company. Everyone had this fear on their faces, the accountant, the data entry clerk, the administrative assistant, the customer service reps, the loan officers, the paralegals and even the lawyers. And so, as expected its time to take the war against the aliens as serious as it can be.

"What's going on here, someone pour the booze, let's get the party started" the boss cheered giving the workers who are about to lose their jobs a last pat on the shoulder.

Introducing AI in the workplace must have been considered by many bosses as a huge improvement and better alternative to human labor. The most cutting-edge and promising area for workplace and workforce management today is thought to be AI. Applications with AI enhancements are now used in 40% of human resources (HR) operations in both small and large businesses throughout the world. Although some European and Asian businesses are joining, the majority of these businesses are based in the United States. More and more international businesses are starting to see the value of AI in assisting personnel management, according to a PricewaterhouseCoopers poll. Furthermore, it is asserted that 32% of human resources departments in tech firms and other organizations are redesigning their organizations with AI's assistance to maximize adaptability and learning and to integrate the insights gained from both technology and employee feedback as effectively as possible. According to a recent study, half of the chief HR officers surveyed are aware of the potential uses of technology in HR for operations, talent acquisition, and development. According to a Deloitte survey, 71% of worldwide companies give people analytics a high priority for their organizations since it should enable them to cope with the so-called "people problem" in addition to providing sound business insights.

Many employers have systematically put AI in charge of the employees. Imagine a number of workers discovering that their activities are being monitored and evaluated by a robot. Yeah, that new employee that tells on everyone is here again. How did workers welcome the idea that they could no longer maneuver working hours, pretend to be at work or run some tricks on the boss? Well, it's time to outperform the silly robots and show the boss who is capable.

In a company that manufactured widgets, there was this guy, Tom who worked on the assembly line. Tom had been working at the company for over twenty years and was proud of his job. However, the company decided to introduce an AI system that could do Tom's job much faster and more efficiently. Tom was determined to keep his job, so he spent weeks trying to learn how the AI system worked and how he could outsmart it. He even went as far as to sabotage the system, hoping it would fail and the company would realize how important human workers were. Unfortunately, Tom's plan backfired. When the AI system malfunctioned, the company lost a lot of money and had to let go of several workers, including Tom. The company realized they couldn't trust their employees to work alongside the AI system, and they decided to fully implement the technology. Tom was devastated. He had lost his job and had no other skills to fall back on. He had put all of his efforts into trying to save his job from the AI system, and it had backfired in the worst way possible.

In another company Sarah worked in customer service. Like Tom, she was faced with the prospect of losing her job to an AI system. She tried to adapt by learning new skills, but the company was determined to replace her with a machine. Sarah refused to give up, and she came up with a plan to show the company how much better she was at customer service than the AI system. She created a customer service challenge, where customers would call in and be helped either by her or the AI system. Unfortunately, the AI system outperformed Sarah in every single call. The customers were more satisfied with the AI system's service, and the company saw no reason to keep Sarah on.

Sarah was devastated. She had tried her best, but it wasn't enough. She learned that sometimes, no matter how hard you try, you can't beat the efficiency and effectiveness of AI systems. In the end, both Tom and Sarah learned a valuable lesson. They realized that technology is constantly advancing, and it's essential to keep learning and growing. While it's important to fight for your job, sometimes it's better to embrace change and look for new opportunities.

After losing in the attempt to overcome AI, workers and people generally resorted to badmouthing the system. A lot of people came out to say so much about how AI is not as good as the employers thought it to be. In a conversation Martin, my favorite cousin had with his boss, the cheap guy tried to sell the system bad to his boss. He started this way.

"You can't expect this thing to ultimately replace me, how are you sure it was not developed by some psychopath motivated by the devil. You don't want some robots coming after your life, do you? "

"And what's your own motivation?" the boss asked? And he continued without letting him answer "because you definitely work like someone without any and you even seem to be after my life, Martin". Jonathan had said.

But these are not the actual wars against AI, the actual war against AI were fought by researchers and business analysts. They put up so much arguments and speculations about how AI might have been created by people who have ulterior motives other than positivity and growth. Some people have come up with conspiracy theories that the inventors who created these awesome systems and have so much control on them can one day have that volume of influence on users. And who knows what they have in plan for users who would have become addicted to the awesome robots and systems that never complain and always gets the job done. He would probably hand over the entire company to bots if they prove effective enough.

The intricacy of the algorithms utilized in AI systems poses a threat to the privacy of individuals and businesses. Increasingly sophisticated AI can base its calculations on anomalies in the data that are invisible to the naked eye. This means that people may not realize certain personal or sensitive56 data is being used to make conclusions about them. Massive volumes of (personal) data are required for AI systems, and if this data is compromised, it can be utilized for criminal activities like identity theft or cyber bullying.

And then people also brought many other allegations such as lack of reality. I mean, we already had to deal with a lot of fake loves here and there but then people claimed that AI would give more room to fallacies and people would utilize this to achieve their evil goals such as social manipulation. Social manipulation is one of the biggest risks of artificial intelligence, according to a

2018 assessment on potential misuse of the technology. As politicians increasingly rely on platforms to advance their agendas, this fear has come to pass. As a recent example, Ferdinand Marcos Jr. used a troll army on TikTok to win the support of younger Filipinos during the 2022 election. TikTok uses an AI algorithm that floods users' newsfeeds with material relevant to previously seen media on the platform. This procedure and the algorithm's failure to weed out hazardous and misleading content are targeted in criticism of the app, casting doubt on TikTok's ability to shield its users from harmful and misleading content.

People who fear about AI have pointed out how deep fakes have infiltrated the political and social realms; online media and news have grown even murkier. The technology makes it simple to swap out a figure's image in a photo or video. As a result, malicious actors now have a new channel for disseminating false information and war propaganda, creating a nightmare situation in which it can be extremely difficult to tell the difference between reliable and false news.

The possibility of bias and discrimination in AI technology is another obstacle it presents according to the people who cared to double check. If the data used to train an AI system is biased, then the final system will also be biased. Because of this, people may be treated differently because of their color, gender, or socioeconomic background. To avoid bias, it is crucial that AI systems be trained using a wide range of data and undergo regular audits. It may not be obvious at first that prejudice and bias in AI have anything to do with personal information being kept private. After all, privacy is typically viewed as an independent concern unconnected to data security or the right to solitude. However, there is a deeper connection between the two problems, and I will explain why. To begin, remember that many forms of AI use data to guide its judgments. This information can be gathered from a wide range of resources, including internet actions, social media posts, and official documents. A person's race, gender, religious affiliation, and political leanings can all be inferred from seemingly trivial information like this. An unfair or even detrimental outcome for humans can result if a biased or prejudiced AI system uses this data to further entrench its biases. Think about a corporation that uses AI to sort through resumes before interviewing candidates. Data concerning a candidate's gender or ethnicity could be used to unfairly rule them out of consideration if the system is prejudiced against women or persons of color. The applicant is harmed, and existing inequities in the labor force are reinforced.

And then there is the talk about privacy and job displacement and it seems to be the major problem here. But many people want to hide the fact that they are just scared for themselves so they fronted the arguments and realities and fallacies first. Researchers claimed that artificial intelligence presents a huge threat due to the possibility of job loss and economic disruption. Increases in the sophistication of AI systems mean that they can take over more and more human activities. Consequently, this may cause people to lose their jobs, disrupt entire sectors, and need them to acquire new skills. However, there are several significant links between the loss of a job and the right to privacy. One negative effect of AI technology on the economy is the greater financial uncertainty it can bring to workers. This, in turn, might cause people to feel pressured to compromise their privacy in order to make ends meet. Consider the case of a worker who has been laid off because of technological advancements. They are so financially strapped that they have no choice but to participate in the gig economy. A person's location, work history, and evaluations from past clients may all need to be shared with a platform in order to obtain work. While this may be necessary in order to get hired, the potential for this information to be shared with third parties or used to target advertisements poses severe privacy concerns.

The gig economy is only one example of an industry where privacy and job security are concerns. This also applies to the ways in which artificial intelligence is implemented during the selection procedure. Some businesses, for instance, utilize AI algorithms to conduct preliminary screenings of job candidates by examining their social media profiles and online behavior. Since prospective employees might not be aware that their personal information is being collected and used in this way, this raises considerations about privacy and concerns about the veracity of the data being used. The loss of employment and economic disruption brought on by AI technology has far-reaching implications for privacy, since it may force some people to give up personal information in order to keep their heads above water. Personal information is becoming more important to corporations in the age of AI, and it is being put to uses we could never have anticipated. Artificial intelligence (AI) is being utilized to collect, process, and analyze our personal information across a wide range of applications, from facial recognition to predictive algorithms. For instance, in recent years generative AI has risen in popularity thanks to its ability to let people generate material that looks and feels like it was made by humans, such as word and image production tools. Generative AI has the potential to revolutionize many industries, but it also poses serious privacy concerns because the corporations that create these tools may gather and analyze the data that users give as input. Personal information, photos, and other forms of sensitive material are just some of the examples of what users may be prompted to enter. Concerns about data security and privacy arise with the benefits of using this information to train and improve generative AI models.

People also worry that evil geniuses would abuse AI technology. This is seen as a major threat. It is possible to employ AI to produce highly realistic false photos and films, which might be used to propagate disinformation or sway public opinion. Phishing assaults, in which users are tricked into divulging personal information or clicking on dangerous links, can also be made more complex with the help of AI. The creation and distribution of fraudulent movies and photos can have severe consequences for individuals' personal security and safety. This is because the actors in these fake media may or may not have given their permission for their likeness to be utilized in this context. The spread of fake news can cause harm to individuals if it is used to spread inaccurate or damaging information about them or if it is employed in a way that compromises their privacy. Take the hypothetical scenario of a malicious actor using AI to fabricate a video of a politician participating in some sort of unethical or unlawful activity. It doesn't matter how obviously false the video is; it might still go viral, doing tremendous damage to the politician's reputation. This is an intrusion into their personal space, and it could even end up harming them.

These and more are the claims that people have put up against AI and I believe these claims have some facts to them. In real time, a lot of people have already been sacked due to the introduction of AI in the workplace. And many have lost their lives or other things of value. We found ourselves struggling day and day to be in charge of our own lives but we have to give way to AI here and there. Well, whose side am I on? I am on the side of the living of course. With AI having the potentials to take over people's jobs and lives. I believe it is important that we learn to manage these aliens so that we can forever be in charge of our own lives. But first, let's take a look into the future of jobs with AI. Let's see what's about to get better and what's about to get worse.

Chapter Three: The AI Impact

Martin again! He came home looking happy and all. "What is the gist?", I asked.

"Well, you gotta see these new apps on my tab. Like, I literally have to nothing myself. My boss has been using these awesome writing tools and today he was willing to share. He had to attend a meeting and he needed some paper works done before going. He had to call me into his office and asked me to access some files. He pointed these apps to me on his computer and I was done in a very short time" he said, laughing like a baby and continued.

"And then, the boss just spends thousands of dollars monthly bringing in these cool machines. I guess the guys down floor are about to get pay cuts too just like me and they are already grumbling about it. Jonathan had sworn to sue them should any of the machines be damaged or get stolen. I wonder what he plans to do with so much machines and robots."

I smiled and said "guess you are just getting used to the robotic and artificial workplace, enjoy".

He looked at me, smirking and raising his eyebrows. I believe he hadn't been aware of the trends of the time despite how much I have tried to bring him up to date with things happening around the world, despite me not leaving the house all day. He had gone past the fear of being replaced and was then faced with the task of adapting to automation in his workplace. Let's take a peep into workplaces and see how artificial intelligence is turning things around for employees and their favorite employers.

Businesses Now with AI

In spite of doomsayers' claims that AI will cause widespread job losses in the near future, the reality is that AI is playing an increasingly important supporting role in the business world, rather than a disruptive one. I have so much interest in the business world. That's the world's biggest deal, isn't it? Imagine AI at the very heart of the world economy. Already, we're in an era of business when rapid, technology-driven transformation is assisting us in meeting a variety of growth-limiting obstacles. The ramifications of AI technology for future growth are substantial. The use of big data analytics is also crucial in making AI suitable for business use. AI has many potential uses as it takes a place next to the development of essential services such as communications, energy, healthcare, agriculture, and education. With the help of AI, start-ups are now able to tackle revenue and popularity issues and acquire a competitive edge in the global market.

According the world renowned Accenture Institute for High Performance, it can be speculated that by 2035, Artificial Intelligence (AI) could double annual economic growth rates in many highly developed and fast developing countries. In the United States, the annual growth rate rose from 2.6% to 4.6% adding up an additional $8.3 Trillion with widespread AI adoption. In the United Kingdom, implementation of AI in the business system could make an increase of $814 Billion in the economy, raising the annual growth rate from 2.5% to about 4%. AI might be a disruption but it is a very big boost.

With the ability to evaluate data across numerous capabilities, detect fraud, and provide first-rate customer relationship management, businesses and sectors that adopt AI applications will expand and diversify business systems across the world. Businesses now use the expansive abilities of AI to their advantage in the market. Artificial intelligence aids in the discovery of answers to difficult commercial challenges. This i Most CEOs still view AI as little more than a curiosity, much like they did with PCs in the 1980s and the Internet in the 1990s. The use of AI has become ubiquitous in the commercial world. Robots, smart automobiles, consumer electronics, etc., as well as numerous apps and business solutions, are just some of the intelligent implementations benefiting from the use of AI and advanced machine learning. Artificial intelligence is now being used to automate many intricate commercial procedures. Significant time savings can be made, and employees' abilities can be put to better use in areas such as ideation, innovation, and research.

Artificial intelligence (AI) now plays a huge role in studying the market and your customers. In order to create a superior and improved product, predictive analysis can be applied to the collected data from the system matrix, the web matrix, and social media. With the help of customer insights, you can improve the quality of the service you provide to your clients. The value of AI to new businesses is enormous. Startups have more leeway to try out novel approaches to problems and develop creative strategies for expansion. Predictive maintenance aids new businesses by lowering maintenance costs through preventative measures.

By delivering the most efficient marketing tool for your organization and by weeding out unlikely prospects from the list of possible clients, AI-based solutions may also optimize marketing tactics and save marketing costs. Many of your clients now do much of their business online, and many of them are active on social media. Important metrics of online social networks can be understood with the help of artificial intelligence. Methods from the field of data mining are being applied to the study of social media activity of all stripes. It is possible to identify the most influential individuals and to categorize the various social marketing strategies.

Artificial intelligence programs are more effective than just statistical methods because they may acquire new knowledge. This enables them to respond to shifting market dynamics and enhance performance over time as new information is gathered. Many businesses already employ or intend to employ AI-powered virtual assistants. Chatbots are used in many different ways by businesses. In terms of business segments, customer service is paramount. Machine-driven help combined with human-driven customer service has potential, but many are still skeptical of the idea because machines can break down at any time. Such like... Questions about a flight's status, alternate flights, schedules, etc., can be easily answered by an AI application designed for use with airlines. This frees up human agents to tackle more intricate issues. Marketers are finding that chatbots are a great method to interact with potential customers. The use of chatbots and other forms of virtual support can have a major impact on the way in which customers interact with technology. We anticipate that more businesses will utilize virtual assistants to provide superior customer support to their clientele in the coming decade.

Cold phoning and lengthy emails are so last century in the sales world. There are a plethora of additional forms of media that impact consumers, from television ads to social media. Snapchat, too, is being used for commercial purposes. Integrating AI into your customer relationship management system (CRM) is a simple yet effective step toward creating new and efficient marketing strategies for your firm. An intelligent customer relationship management system can take care of every aspect of your company's operations. Artificial intelligence is being used by sales teams to better understand their clients and provide individualized services. With the help of AI, e-commerce businesses are able to ask customers a series of questions about their shopping habits and personal tastes in order to tailor their recommendations to each individual. The potential for conversion will improve if this is done. Without a shadow of a doubt, artificial intelligence is improving sales as we know it by revolutionizing sales processes. Untailored solutions are no longer provided to customers. As a result, businesses see increased conversion rates and faster access to client data.

AI now let's business owners customize consumer experiences. AI analyzes massive data faster. It can swiftly recognize trends like past buying history, buying preferences, credit ratings, and others. Daily analysis of millions of transactions can customize customer assistance. Businesses may analyze buyer behavior before, during, and after purchase using actionable sales intelligence. This lets businesses personalize every connection and engage customers. Predictive intelligence can improve consumer engagement. An AI-driven application may personalize the sales cycle to engage the appropriate clients with the right material at the right time. AI can help companies identify potential customers. They know the buyer's background before talking to them, making the sales process go smoothly.

The incorporation of AI into the business community has made it possible for smaller businesses to adopt tried and true commercial strategies in order to accomplish more ambitious professional objectives. AI is continually giving start-up companies with a competitive advantage, while large corporations are providing the platform upon which novel solutions can be constructed. The use of artificial intelligence (AI) has become ubiquitous in today's world, whether it be in the form of a robot in a production facility, self-driving cars, or a voice-activated resource in complex medical procedures.

AI in the Media Industry

All speakers in the AI-related dialogues are in agreement that AI has great promise for a variety of societal and economic benefits. The media can't be ignored here. With the advent of digital transformation, the media landscape has seen dramatic shifts. We have been offering media software testing services for a long time, and in that time we have seen AI emerge as a game-changing technology that has altered the media landscape forever. This blog post will explain why artificial intelligence (AI) is the wave of the future in the news industry.

The impact that digital media is having on the industry is staggering. All market actors in the media sector, from radio and TV to film, have emphasized the need of having digital strategies and how these strategies may become key sources of revenue generating. Artificial intelligence (AI) can help media companies undertake the challenging digital transition they hope for in order to preserve a competitive advantage or surpass the competition. Unbeknownst to us, media players' business models already incorporated several services made possible by artificial intelligence. Take Netflix as an illustration. It uses computer vision algorithms to power its recommendation engine, which helps users rate movies before they've even seen them. Similarly, 20th Century Fox and IBM used AI to make a terrifying and enticing teaser. All you have to do is press play. The last example is achievable thanks to the application of machine learning ML algorithms by IBM and 20th Century Fox, who analyzed several trailers for thrillers and horror films in order to produce a single, highly effective teaser.

In today's digitally enabled climate, media and entertainment organizations communicate with viewers utilizing a data-driven strategy. Their brand recognition is strong, and their social media profiles are engaging. Data mining and predictive models have helped gamers gain a deeper understanding of their target demographic. It has a wide range of applications in a wide variety of settings and procedures. At first glance, it seems to be useful for helping media companies enhance their customers' experiences. Artificial intelligence is used for a variety of purposes in this area, including predictive analytics, recommendation algorithms, lead scoring, audience segmentation, customer journey mapping, and so on. Apps powered by AI are helping to increase content quality and reach a wider audience.

It's all about becoming specific. One of the most exciting ways AI is reshaping the media industry is by helping media companies manage user behavior and make personalized content recommendations. Better consumer satisfaction and involvement are other benefits of cognitive AI. These days, if you use an OTT service, you can get recommendations on what to watch next. Artificial intelligence is employed to make these suggestions based on our viewing habits.

Media players also leverage AI to enhance their offerings. All of this is made feasible by AI-enabled technology through the automation of editorials, the removal of manual involvement, and the optimization of the cost of content development. Using AI and sophisticated algorithms, production companies and other media organizations can create convincing yet engaging advertising campaigns and marketing strategies, such as promotion, design, advertisements, etc. By employing predictive analytics principles, AI can also speed up marketing processes. Two of AI's biggest benefits for the media industry are its ability to manage intellectual property and royalties and to acquire digital rights for content. This frees them up to focus on picking out new and exciting material. The system also facilitates the identification of outliers in subscriber and fan engagement data. Furthermore, it eliminates human labor from the formerly manual processes of captioning, filtering, and distributing news. Live film generated by AI, for instance, can help record the enthusiastic response of the crowd to each goal and the exciting play of the game. It can be used in tandem with in-game imagery to create an engaging story that, hey, guess what? The greater the content's virility, the more people will watch it.

One of the most remarkable ways in which AI is helping the media industry is by identifying false stories. Today, fake news may be identified using deep learning AI algorithms that can trace a story's origins and verify its accuracy. One way that AI is being put to use in the entertainment industry is through chatbots. Reaching Out to Customers using Chatbots

Conversational bots powered by AI allow businesses to interact with customers around the clock and on a wider scale. As a result, the total CX was enhanced. They make the browsing experience more convenient and enjoyable. Chatbots can learn from user actions to provide information such as the latest news, weather forecasts, and recommendations for TV shows, movies, and events.

Metadata tagging, like text annotation, entails applying tags to the material or its many parts. Imagine there are a million new pieces of content created every minute, and humans are unable to organize all of this content into digestible categories. Employees at media companies must spend endless hours consuming content in order to manually categorize products, locations, and situations and apply tags. The process would take a very long time. But now, owing to AI, producers can easily assess any media source, recognize things, and tag them with the appropriate tags, making their work immediately discoverable by millions of people. Predicting how users will act and make decisions is an essential part of any company's strategy nowadays. Providing AI-powered services in real time could greatly improve the user experience. Currently, streaming accounts for over half of all global data traffic. Successful AI-backed recommendation systems have already been implemented by OTT providers like Prime Video and Netflix. Thus, the same may be expected from the subsequent wave of digital video.

Virtual reality (VR) and augmented reality (AR) are also seeing widespread use. A 2017 analysis predicts that virtual reality will be one of the media industry's most lucrative niches. The interactive character of media companies' content can be freely explored with AR/VR content, improving the user experience. Increasing rivalry in the media industry has heightened the necessity for businesses in the industry to find ways to differentiate themselves from the competitors. It is predicted that in the future years, the media industry will undergo a dramatic shift due to the role that artificial intelligence (AI) plays in increasing productivity and producing revenue. But it's just as important for development companies to maximize the benefits of quality assurance. The media industry is a prime illustration of AI's usefulness, as evidenced by the aforementioned applications. These examples demonstrate how businesses are prepared to take advantage of and experiment with AI's potential to boost company performance through enhanced customer experience and value creation.

Oh! Robots in Healthcare?

Today's technological advancements, regardless of industry, aim to save time, boost efficiency, and improve company and consumer outcomes. The expanding application of artificial intelligence (AI) in health care shows how innovation and medicine are affecting providers and patients. AI is enabling complex computations, analyses, and research breakthroughs. AI frees up time for doctors to interact with patients, make discoveries, and provide better treatment.

But how? AI improves health care in various ways. Algorithms and software analyze, analyze, and comprehend complex medical and health care data to improve treatment options and outcomes. AI can now make decisions without human input. Machine learning, an AI subfield, is vital to health care applications. Health practitioners may design novel medical techniques, manage huge patient data and records, and improve chronic illness therapy with machine learning.

Natural language processing (NLP), a second but equally essential subset of AI, makes it easier than ever to automate many of the complicated, time-consuming, repetitive operations that drain health care administration resources. Health care businesses can drastically improve efficiency and accuracy in important areas with NLP. According to a HIMSS article, natural language processing improves outcomes and helps doctors provide more individualized treatment. NLP can translate clinical notes in EHRs, allowing clinicians to enter data once. NLP and AI-enabled software may access medical imaging, EHR data, and consumer devices like activity trackers, cellphones, and connected medical equipment. Clinicians have more diagnostic and therapeutic choices, improving care.

AI and machine learning in healthcare have an adoption curve like other technologies. The COVID-19 pandemic has accelerated the adoption of these technologies, which are used in various health care fields. Today, patient data manages care and informs future therapies. Without AI, data hasn't led to medical breakthroughs. In a recent HIMSS article, Google Brain AI Research Group product manager Lily Peng, MD, PhD, said, "while human intelligence is best suited for integrating small numbers of very large effect factors, AI is particularly adept at combing through and identifying patterns in vast numbers and obscure factors."

WakeMed Health & Hospitals senior vice president, chief quality and medical staff officer Chris DeRienzo, MD, MPP, FAAP, sees another benefit in using patient data to improve treatment. "The key benefits of artificial intelligence are grounded in this ability to continuously comb the electronic medical records (EMR), training on past patients' trajectories in the same way clinicians are trained and hone the lenses of their prescription glasses, patient by patient by the millions."

Reimbursement requires complete, timely, and accurate paperwork. Documentation gaps can cause erroneous coding that lowers revenue and slows or stops reimbursement. Documentation issues can hinder cash flow. Documentation errors cost money to fix. Documentation and coding issues now threaten revenue more than they did a few years ago. New risk-based models have complicated documentation, coding, and payment procedures. As reimbursement models change, quality events must be appropriately reported based on clinical data. Revenue and quality reporting to the Centers for Medicare and Medicaid Services (CMS) are public information, and ratings and penalties can affect community view of the health care provider. Intelligent automation that discovers documentation gaps and improves documentation at the point of care promotes accurate quality reporting, correct coding, efficient downstream revenue cycle procedures, and proper revenue capture.

The U.S. National Institutes of Health defines precision medicine as "an emerging approach for disease treatment and prevention that takes into account individual variability in genes, environment, and lifestyle for each person." AI can improve precision medicine's ability to tailor therapy and prevention to each patient.

AI and machine learning can digest data quickly to produce useful results, as indicated above. Precision medicine requires fast "mining and analyzing large quantities of genetic, clinical, social, lifestyle and preference data across broad, heterogenous populations," according to Dixie B. Baker, PhD, FHIMSS, senior partner, Martin, Blanck and Associates. Administrative inefficiency wastes $91 billion in health care costs annually. Thankfully, this area of health care operations can integrate AI and machine learning techniques without much disruption.

AI can automate billing, patient check-in, filing, data input, and more. AI lets a health system focus its most precious resources—providers and health care professionals—on care. AI is revolutionizing clinical decision-making as well as research and diagnosis. AI systems can "learn" from limitless data sets and find patterns, which is improving many therapeutic fields. AI and machine learning also enable more individualized medical care. Consider all the data AI can harness, from genomic, biomarker, and phenotypic data to health records and delivery systems. HIMSS said the system supports judgments in data-intensive fields like radiology, pathology, and ophthalmology.

AI is determining a patient's hospital stay. This enhances decision-making, care planning, and patient management, preventing problems, improving patient outcomes, and lowering health care costs. IBM Watson is helping researchers find better cancer treatments. IBM Watson for Genomics identified approximately 1,000 patient treatments at the University of North Carolina Lineberger Comprehensive Cancer Center. AI-powered solutions analyzed vast data to find better treatments for genetically aberrant tumor patients.

Google Cloud Healthcare API data was used to create an AI system to reduce readmissions and hospital stays. Through machine learning, Google Cloud AI was able to leverage patient EHR data to help doctors make better clinical decisions. Avicenna from IBM can read and identify anomalies in medical pictures like CT scans and X-rays. It can even prescribe treatment by comparing results to medical records. Avicenna analyzes medical photos using a variety of image-processing methods. Some are trained to determine how far down a patient's chest a CT scan slice is from. Others can recognize organs or blood clots."

Health care will always involve human-to-human touch, notwithstanding medical technology's tremendous advances. However, AI helps health care practitioners across disciplines learn and grow. AI frees healthcare physicians to focus on patients by automating monotonous duties. Patients can now take a more active role in their health treatment thanks to the IoT, backed by AI and machine learning. Technology-driven patient engagement options include online EHR access and wearable device data sharing.

Harvard Medical School uses AI-enabled proactive patient interaction. They now use an AI-powered chatbot to diagnose and treat patients faster. Buoy Health lets people talk to a bot about their symptoms. Based on health data and understanding, the app can then steer the person to the right treatment. AI-powered engagement improves communication between health care practitioners and patients, leading to more tailored care. AI processing and increased patient data sharing give doctors better insight into symptom patterns and treatment techniques that improve patient outcomes. "Unlocking data [on health conditions] that historically we've made simple decisions about, AI allows us to get much deeper and look for associations the human brain isn't able to do... but a computer can," said Dr. David B. Agus, MD.

AI's impact on healthcare will only increase. AI is currently driving pharmacological, diagnostic, and health care breakthroughs. However, current technology suggests that AI will eventually be an essential aspect of daily health care, benefiting patients and medical facilities.

Business Insider Intelligence estimates 30% of health care expenditures are administrative. AI can pre-authorize insurance, follow up on outstanding payments, and keep records. AI-powered kiosks may even check patients in at hospitals and clinics. AI lightens workloads so more time can be spent on value-added tasks, not replacing jobs. Health industry professionals think AI will harvest marketing data. If I buy hiking boots online, insect spray and sunscreen are suggested. "The data analytics behind those recommendations includes a wealth of information about me—my demographics, such as age, gender, education, income level, where I live, and other factors that influence my buying decisions," said Mark Weber, senior vice president, Infor Health Solutions. "I expect to apply the same principles to healthcare data to improve patient outcomes, costs, and efficiencies."

AI—specifically NLP—will enhance evidence-based medicine. Natural language processing is used to find missing medical records, but it may soon be used to find treatment or diagnosis errors. Many researchers believe clinically intelligent NLP will allow AI to detect misdirected care or ineffective treatment and inform clinicians. Patient outcomes and readmissions will improve. Triage functions are another AI-driven breakthrough. Health informatics-driven triage function algorithms on wearable devices will warn patients in real time. A device that identifies an odd medical occurrence can alert the wearer and call a doctor or hospital. Health care providers aim to improve patient care and results. More health care workers are enrolling in health informatics, data science, or both disciplines to fulfill that purpose. The University of San Diego's Health Care Informatics master's program combines health informatics and data science to prepare students to create innovative, data-driven health care solutions.

Alien Footprints in the Financial Sector Too?

Many assume block chain, crypto currencies, and Robo-advisors will alter finance, but AI will. It is already revolutionizing other industries, and the finance industry needs to catch up. Artificial intelligence in banking Digitization, the deployment of AI-enabled solutions, and digital transformations are all on the rise in the global banking business, and this trend shows no signs of slowing down. The potential for the financial services sector to use AI-based solutions is growing as time goes on. The advantages of these AI technologies are well known in the banking and finance industries. The incorporation of AI-based solutions is a current pattern in the financial sector. Artificial intelligence (AI) technologies will help banks make sense of the massive amounts of data they create, transform how they interact with their customers, and ultimately improve service quality. Financial services is huge and complicated. It includes retail banking, investment management, insurance, and accounting. AI boosts productivity and cuts costs in various ways due to the industry's size. As companies seek to improve customer experience and efficiency, AI is increasingly used in finance.

Some AI-based solutions have already seen substantial adoption by financial organizations. Chatbots in the front office and anti-payments fraud systems in the back office are where most organizations start when implementing AI technologies. With the help of AI technology, financial institutions can provide customers with seamless support around the clock. It is possible that the back and middle offices of investment banking and other financial institutions, in addition to retail banking, will use AI solutions in the near future. Artificial intelligence (AI) is currently being used by financial institutions to cut expenses in three primary areas: front office (conversational banking), middle office (anti-fraud), and back office (underwriting). Banks can save a significant amount of money using AI-based solutions for front and middle office tasks.

By 2027, banks may save $447 billion with AI. The fintech business is increasingly adopting digital—global banks' IT budgets will reach $297 billion by 2021, according to the report. Financial firms employ this technology to automate customer service and detect fraud. AI will continue to transform financial services. AI is transforming financial services in these areas. Predictive models help banks spot fraud by anticipating loan defaulters. Deep learning predicts market volatility and trades instantly. NLP can answer simple questions or execute complex transactions using voice commands or mobile typing. Machine learning can estimate customer preferences and recommend products without making mistakes under pressure or fatigue.

Front-end AI implementation in the banking industry is helping to standardize the user identification and authentication process, make banking services available 24/7 via chatbots and voice assistants, strengthen relationships with customers, and offer more tailored insights. In order to better detect and prevent payments fraud and to improve the processes for AML and KYC regulatory checks, banks are adopting AI technologies within their middle office activities. In response to new challenges and rising client demands, the banking and financial services sector has adopted AI technologies.

While the banking sector is gradually moving its activities online, it is still heavily reliant on manual, paper-based procedures. Because of the high probability of error associated with manual operations, banks incur high operational costs. In the banking business, robotic process automation (RPA) can be used to replace labor-intensive, error-prone procedures like compiling customer databases from paper-based sources including contracts, forms, and other documents. In the banking industry, various workflows were formerly controlled manually, but now AI-based technologies like enhanced handwriting recognition, natural language processes, and others handle these tasks.

Customers typically avoid banking hours due to the lengthy procedures involved. Sometimes you'll have to get by when the banks are closed for the day because of a holiday or the weekend. Here, AI-based solutions are altering the landscape. The use of chatbots, or conversational assistants, is one of AI's primary benefits. Customers have grown accustomed to interacting with chatbots for questions and routine banking procedures, which formerly needed face-to-face human interaction, because they are available around the clock. These chatbots have been around for a while, but their popularity was boosted by the global pandemic's emergence. Chatbots are increasingly being used by financial institutions to inform customers about services beyond those specifically requested by the customer. Chatbots can use artificial intelligence (AI) tools like machine learning (ML) and predictive analytics to provide highly personalized services to customers in real time about the banks' new offerings and products, resulting in increased revenue for the banks and a better overall experience for the customers.

One area where these cutting-edge technologies excel beyond human capabilities is in the detection of fraud. These AI-based technologies can assist with the algorithmic processing of large databases. Advanced algorithms are being used by the financial sector to enhance data collection and analysis. In addition, banking is one of the most strictly regulated economic sectors worldwide. In order to prevent widespread defaults and fraud, governments employ a variety of rules aimed at ensuring that financial institutions have acceptable risk profiles. In addition, these rules prevent banking clients from exploiting financial institutions for illegal purposes. Banks use AI based solutions to monitor transactions, customer behaviors, and audit information according to various compliance and regulatory standards due to the high cost and even higher liability associated with noncompliance.

To make safer, more lucrative, and more well-informed credit and lending choices, financial institutions are turning to AI-based solutions. Many financial institutions today still rely only on things like credit reports, user references, banking activity, etc. when determining an applicant's or company's creditworthiness. These credit reporting systems aren't foolproof; they have their biases and inaccuracies, and they may fail to include some of your past transactions, leading to incorrect labeling of your creditors. In order to predict whether or not a customer with a thin credit file will default, AI-based systems can analyze not only the available data but also the customer's past actions and patterns.

And the emerging Fintech is not getting left out. Fintech companies use AI for many reasons. First, AI can process vast amounts of data faster than humans. Fintech companies must make decisions based on continuously changing data. AI can assist finance developers customize services for each user. Fintech organizations may customize consumer experiences by studying their needs and preferences. AI can assist the financial services industry keep ahead of the competition. As more fintech companies enter the market, those that can use AI to differentiate will certainly prosper.

To keep ahead of the competition and meet customer expectations, the financial sector is always changing. AI will transform finance quicker than any other area for years. It powers current trading systems, reduces risk and compliance costs, and improves all customer-facing channels, from phone to online chat. AI will increasingly improve the financial sector as technology advances.

Did We Let AI into Governance?

A lot of money is being spent by several nations to improve their AI capacities. For instance, in order to compete with China and the United States, French President Emmanuel Macron declared in March 2018 that France would invest $1.8 billion in its AI sector. Vladimir Putin, the president of Russia, also said in public that "whoever becomes the leader in this sector [AI] will become the ruler of the world," alluding to a significant Russian investment in the development of this technology. Other nations, including South Korea, have also committed significantly more money to AI.

Do you know that the Russian meddling in the U.S. election process has put the topic of cyber protection front and center in the headlines. Governments must have access to technologies that can counteract increasingly complex types of attack. NVIDIA, a technology company, and Booz Allen Hamilton, a consulting firm, have partnered to develop machine learning and deep learning technologies for improved cyber threat detection. The consequence will be a more robust national cyber defense and less room for foreign influence in democratic processes.

Cyber-attacks pose a serious threat to vital infrastructure and private information. Many government organizations have begun deploying AI-based network traffic monitoring and threat prevention solutions as a means of addressing this issue. This provides further defense against malicious software and phishing attempts. AI can encrypt private information to make it more difficult for hackers to access, in addition to defending against external cyber threats. By bolstering the safety of sensitive information, government entities may ensure the uninterrupted operation of their computer systems and networks.

Now talking about the actual road traffic, managing traffic is one of the most difficult tasks facing governments and urban planners today, making AI a promising solution. Machine learning and computer vision are two examples of

AI that are now being used to analyze traffic data for patterns, allowing authorities to pinpoint congested regions and implement fixes. Using previous data, AI might determine the most likely locations for bottlenecks to form, such as in the event of road closures or accidents. Using AI for traffic management has offered many advantages beyond just facilitating smoother traffic flow. One way it can lessen urbanization's impact is by making commutes faster and more efficient. Reduced idling time in traffic means less pollution and fewer greenhouse gas emissions.

Congestion in urban areas is a common problem that can be difficult for authorities to manage. One contributing factor is the surprising unpredictability of traffic congestion. Even if you avoid driving during rush hour, you may still experience significant delays throughout the day. In a fascinating paper from 2016, researchers report that using deep learning techniques to predict near-term traffic conditions yielded a 90 percent accuracy rate. When authorities and those in charge of traffic control have better insight into what the future holds, they can take preventative measures to reduce congestion in a city's most congested transportation hubs.

Immigration application processing is also being sped up with the help of Ai. Artificial intelligence is so appealing because it can automate tasks that humans would otherwise have to complete manually. The procedures involved in applying for and processing visas and immigration documents are a major source of stress for government immigration and naturalization services. Because each case takes so long to process, immigration offices frequently face substantial backlogs. While human civil servants are still responsible for making the ultimate decision in each case, AI now shine in this context by automating some of the processing.

AI really has many potential applications in government, but one of the most exciting is its potential to aid law enforcement through the analysis of surveillance footage, the tracking of social media accounts, and other similar activities. This is a long-standing issue for law enforcement, which often lacks the personnel and technology to sift through massive amounts of data or keep tabs on a huge number of suspects. Machine learning algorithms and image recognition tools are just two examples of the artificial intelligence technologies that are helping law enforcement organizations better analyze surveillance footage, identify criminal trends on social media, and track down suspects. Governments can benefit from the ongoing development of facial recognition software by using it to track down fleeing criminals, while state police forces can make use of the powerful machine learning and deep learning algorithms that have revolutionized image detection and classification. The software works by analyzing photographs from CCTV and other sources over an area where the suspect is thought to be present, leading to a more confident identification.

By freeing up time and resources that would have been spent on lower priority cases, this not only helps to speed the process of discovering offenders, but also allows law enforcement organizations to focus on investigating more serious crimes.

And then there's the task of the tax office. The sheer volume of data that needs to be evaluated to identify potential cases of tax evasion or fraud is one of the fundamental challenges of tax collecting. There may be a high cost in time and effort as well as in the skills and manpower needed to complete this task successfully. Automating this task with AI requires the analysis of massive amounts of financial and other relevant data using sophisticated data analytics and machine learning methods.

Artificial intelligence can aid governments in the detection of tax evasion and fraud by spotting patterns and trends within this data.

The detection and prevention of fraud and abuse in benefits administration is another important difficulty that governments combat with the use of AI in administration. Government organizations can lose a lot of money if people file false or abusive claims, and as a result, fewer resources will go to those who actually need them. Fortunately, AI systems can sift through mountains of data in search of telltale signs of fraud. These systems might, for instance, examine bank records, employee files, and other datasets in search of anomalies or suspicious trends that would indicate wrongdoing. This could aid government entities in identifying potential sources of fraud and preventing it from happening.

And AI in Education

No sector is left out in this alien invasion and one would expect the academia to be the avengers who save the world. But they are not. AI is currently being used unapologetically in the education sector in a wide range of operations. And teachers now have a new life which is quite different from the boring eye bitched face down lifestyles from repetitive and monotonous work life. The most boring part of the world's most boring job is now being automated and teachers are basking in the euphoria of their newly discovered peace. The educational workforce is beginning to feel the effects of AI.

Data collected from pupils can be analyzed by AI-powered systems to tailor lessons to each individual's needs. Therefore, educators must adjust to utilizing these resources and analyzing the data they provide in order to design effective lessons.

By analyzing student data, technologies powered by AI can reveal patterns and offer insights into each student's learning style, strengths, and limitations. As a result, educators will be better able to develop specialized lesson plans for each student. To ensure that each student is sufficiently pushed to make progress without being overwhelmed, AI-powered adaptive learning systems may now alter the pace and difficulty of learning materials based on the student's progress. This has the potential to keep pupils enthusiastic and involved. Additional learning resources, such as videos, articles, and quizzes, are now being suggested to students using AI-powered recommendation engines. As a result, students are able to tailor their education to their interests and strengths.

Additional learning resources, such as videos, articles, and quizzes, are now being suggested to students using AI-powered recommendation engines. As a result, students are able to tailor their education to their interests and strengths. Further, virtual assistants powered by AI can aid students with assignments, inquiries, and evaluations. This can help students get the help they need right away, even when school is not in session. Grading assignments and giving instant feedback to students is now being automated by AI-powered solutions. This can free up time for educators to concentrate on creating individualized programs for each student's education.

Essays, tasks, and even examinations are being graded by AI systems. As a result, educators may need to prioritize test design and development over grading. Multiple-choice questions, quizzes, and even essays can now be automatically graded by AI-powered systems by assessing content, language, and other characteristics. This can help teachers save time and provide greater grading consistency between courses and/or sections. Artificial intelligence (AI) can instantly evaluate students' responses and make personalized suggestions. Grammar, punctuation, and sentence structure are just some of the areas that can benefit from an AI-powered writing tool. With the use of AI-powered plagiarism detection systems, educators may check student work for instances of possible plagiarism. The data collected from students, such as their grades and test scores, can be analyzed by AI to shed light on how well they are doing in school. Teachers can then tailor their lessons to the areas in which their students are having the most difficulty. To ensure that each student is challenged without becoming overwhelmed, AI-powered evaluations can modify the complexity and tempo of questions based on their previous responses.

Attendance tracking, record keeping, and timetable creation are just some of the administrative duties that can be automated by AI-powered technologies in the educational sector. Because of this, it's possible that administrative personnel will need to learn how to use these programs. Teachers are also benefiting from AI's ability to automate duties like grading student work, spotting problem areas, and making recommendations for pedagogical refinements. Data from multiple sources, including student information systems, learning management systems, and assessment data, is now being automatically collected and processed using AI-powered tools. Time is being saved and data accuracy is increased as a result of this.

In order to aid teachers and school administrators in analyzing large data sets and making intelligent choices, they are turning to data visualization tools powered by artificial intelligence. In order to better forecast future outcomes, AI can now utilize predictive analytics. For instance, AI can be used to help spot children who are at risk of leaving out or who are having academic difficulties, so that educators can step in and aid. A now facilitates more efficient data collecting, visualization, and insights in the field of education. Informed decisions by teachers and principals can boost learning outcomes and academic success for all students.

Well, it's clearly obvious that AI has now changed how things are being done in almost every work of life. Everyone who wants to enjoy their job and their lives generally in the future must learn to adapt to and leverage the different touches of AI in works across the globe. I recently caught my cousin looking through my laptop. I wonder what he was looking for but I know it has to something to do with software that could finish a churn of work in split seconds. And I am sure he would find it. No matter what you do, there is one or more ways you can put one or more AI systems to use to make your work life better.

The fear that AI would take people's job is quite exaggerated and then, not many people are talking about the jobs that would be created by AI. The world as it is evolved would require the use of AI the more and this would breed a new generation of workers in a new and very demanding niche. What job have the aliens brought for humanity in their crazy spaceship? Let's find out.

Chapter Four: Emerging Jobs with AI

AI has not only changed how things are being done in the workplace, it is expanding the workplaces and changing the workforce as well. AI has transformed the world and has opened new channels for people to make a living. The technology is breeding a new generation of workers and a new range of careers and paths through which people have begun to advance over the years. New jobs are showing up on the radar and the cool thing about it is that these jobs are overtaking other jobs which have enjoyed the fame of careers in the past decades. People used to pay so much attention on people in the business sector, health sector and engineering sector. However, AI is revolutionizing the career scopes for emerging workers and it is opening more opportunities to them. The application of artificial intelligence is rapidly spreading into dozens of new industries, which in turn is producing a large number of new job opportunities and making many firms more productive. If you are a student or a recent graduate and you are interested in starting a career in artificial intelligence (AI), you can rest assured that there are plenty of opportunities for you in an industry that is expanding, stable, and always needs qualified IT graduates to get these jobs done. You may take comfort in this fact.

It goes without saying that artificial intelligence is currently pervasive, and the demand for AI specialists, particularly those with relevant expertise and skills, continues to rise. According to Bernard Marr, a business and technology expert to governments and organizations, we now have access to more data than ever before, which implies that artificial intelligence has become smarter, faster, and more accurate AI is the new gold and everyone is trying to catch up.

And the funny part here is that everyone now wants to get in. Even Martin!

He was like "what's machine learning. You must know it. You are the computer guy".

"And what will you do with machine learning?" I asked.

"Well, for a start, I am looking build some awesome apps." he answered with the enthusiasm of a school boy just invited to join a game. He continued "I could be an AI person you know"

"And what does an AI person do?"

"Well, I guess it's about how to train machines to learn, you tell me, I don't know so much about that shit everyone is talking about, believe me. I am blank on this."

"Let me fill you in"

AI has many job opportunities beyond machine learning and software engineering. We are talking multi-millionaire projects and lucrative careers.

Robotics Engineering

Have you ever given any attention to the countless opportunities that come with the creation, installation, testing, and maintenance of your very own robot? Robotics engineers are in great demand because the skill sets they bring to the table come with a variety of benefits that are attractive to a variety of sectors. You might play a role in the development of the next awesome robot product, which will emphasize the creation and upkeep of automated devices, as well as the use of machine learning. If you are good with numbers and want a satisfying career, robotics engineering is vital in manufacturing, agriculture, health care, food preparation, and the military, so this is guaranteed to offer you job security, satisfaction, and the possibility to do something wonderful for many. Robotics engineering is essential in manufacturing, agriculture, health care, food preparation, and the military. The average annual salary of a robotics engineer in the US is $100,000.

Software Engineering

Do you want to do more than merely repair computer systems, but you have exceptional problem-solving skills? In the field of information technology, becoming a software engineer is an established professional path that is now in high demand. This is the foundation upon which the technology that we use today is built. To put it more simply, these experts' area of expertise is in the construction of software. Which is better: Google Chrome or Microsoft Office? Made by software engineers. Software engineers have the knowledge and abilities necessary to develop functional programs for businesses, which constantly require cutting-edge software to supply to clients in order to satisfy their requirements.

Building software that incorporates speech recognition, machine learning, and the end-user system as a whole is one way for software engineers to break into the artificial intelligence field. It is not uncommon for professionals in this field to be responsible not only for the production of software but also for its maintenance and ongoing updates.

This is an essential part of artificial intelligence and the basis for developing software that will influence a large number of people and assist them traverse difficult technologies. A wonderful illustration of this may be seen in Cortana. Imagine you have the ability to create your very own personal virtual assistant. The average annual salary of a software engineer is the $120,000

Computer Vision Engineering

Do you have a decent ability to visualize the information that is presented to you? Engineers specializing in computer vision concentrate mostly on algorithms and visual data; huge corporations such as Apple want their services. They make use of artificial intelligence and contribute to its development in addition to using it.

Computer vision engineering includes the processes of hazard detection in self-driving cars, facial recognition, and even content management on social media websites such as Facebook, to name just a few examples of its applications. Automated algorithms are created and maintained through the process of computer vision engineering.

All of these things have an automated system that is somewhat comparable to artificial intelligence, and it is reasonable to anticipate that within the next few years, the field of artificial intelligence will develop and become increasingly popular. This is a wonderful vocation to consider pursuing if the idea of working with data while consuming it in the form of video feeds, analog visuals, or digital signals appeals to you. The average annual salary of a computer vision engineer in the US is $160,000.

Machine Learning Engineering

An expert in machine learning engineer develops algorithms and models to analyze and draw conclusions from massive datasets. Most careers for machine learning engineers will entail some combination of designing, building, developing, and implementing machine learning models. Machine learning engineers work closely with software engineers and data scientists to design and implement complex algorithms and systems.

In the United States, a machine learning engineer can expect to earn a median yearly salary of $ 100,000.

Natural Language Learning Engineering

Professionals in the field of natural language processing (NLP) use specialized software and hardware, such as speech recognition and text-to-speech engines, to train computers to understand and interpret human language. Engineers specializing in natural language processing (NLP) are responsible for transforming humans' unstructured voice and writing into a form that computers can comprehend. They work closely with other engineers to develop systems that can understand spoken and written language and respond appropriately.

In the United States, a computer vision engineer may expect an average annual pay of $120,000.

Deep Learning Engineer

A deep learning engineer is one of the many interesting careers available in the AI industry. Engineers working in deep learning use a variety of approaches to teach computers algorithms that give them the ability to learn from large datasets. Together with data scientists and other technologists, deep learning engineers create and implement complex neural networks and other deep learning methods.

In the United States, a deep learning engineer can expect to make an average of $150,000 per year.

Data Scientist

This is in no way comparable to the role of a computer vision engineer. If you are skilled at arranging data as well as keeping track of it, you may find satisfaction in a vocation that is utilized by a variety of different businesses. Data collection and transformation into a format that can give the following is the responsibility of a data scientist. Those who are in need will receive insight on speculating on future events and making sure that these data are useful to businesses.

Another significant undertaking for data scientists is the correction of corrupted data or the screening of information that is being processed by the system. This activity is essential to the operation of artificial intelligence systems. This is an excellent option for someone who has an analytical mind and enjoys working with data because it combines the two! The regular annual take home of a data scientist in the United States is $100,000.

Big Data Engineering

Do you believe you are capable of working with information on a greater scale? Engineers specializing in big data are responsible for the design and maintenance of enormous data processing systems. AI will analyze and handle the data relevant to how consumers want AI to be delivered, and these engineers will be essential to the process of managing the massive inflow of data that will be coming in.

Because there is a shortage of skilled individuals, there is a huge demand for people to work in this industry, and it is an ideal choice for anyone who appreciates mathematics or is analytical. Do you have an interest in expanding your knowledge in technological fields that place an emphasis on numbers? Take a look at some of the most popular occupations in data science. Big data engineers earn a goal average annual income of $130,000.

Data Analysis

Analyzing the patterns that emerge in data over the course of time is the primary focus of a data analyst, which is a role that is quite analogous to that of a data scientist. In general, there is less accountability, but the work includes making use of current data rather than creating projections and predictions. This is a popular position that is utilized by a great number of businesses in order to examine the never-ending stream of information that they take in on a daily basis.

For instance, if you would like to aid an AI program and its existing potential for clients, you can be of great assistance to people who are looking to increase their operations. Because AI is constantly used to discover patterns and gather data, there is a strong demand for data analysts. This is because AI is utilized in positions that do not include the creation of AI, but nonetheless use it. The average annual salary of a data analyst in the US is $100,000.

AI Ethicists

There have been a lot of people wondering if artificial intelligence is really a disruptive technology, and AI ethicists are here to make sure that it is used in the right way. These individuals have the primary job of programming opinions, beliefs, political ideals, and general good behaviors into AI in order to avoid AI from acting in bad ways, which could end up having catastrophic effects for a large number of enterprises. This is an excellent line of work to pursue if you have an interest in influencing the actions and decisions that AI makes. Consider reading up on the ethical benefits and drawbacks of AI art generating if you're interested in this subject. This can even inspire you to find a job in the relevant industry. AI ethicists earn an average salary of around $100,000-$130,000 per year.

UX Designer or Developer

Do you also have a good eye for design in addition to your amazing skills in programming? It is the responsibility of a UX Designer, also known as a user experience designer or developer, to craft the manner in which an individual interacts with the application or website that they are now utilizing. This encompasses everything that can be seen and interacted with, even the most basic elements like buttons.

A website or piece of software is completely reimagined from the ground up with the user experience in mind from the very beginning. For instance, a program geared toward seniors would be made to be stress-free and simple to navigate. In the field of artificial intelligence, this would include the manner in which the user interacts with the system, be it in the form of software or hardware, such as robots. Imagine being a contributor to the development of an easy-to-use household robot that doesn't require a lot of commands. The average annual salary of a UX developer on a global scale is $100,000.

Artificial Intelligence Research Scientist

A researcher in artificial intelligence is someone who comes up with novel problems that AI can answer. They conduct innovative studies and create innovative AI technology that companies can employ to streamline their operations. The role of a research scientist in artificial intelligence is to explore the limits of the field. Research scientists show the usefulness of a new tool or product before a corporation spends millions developing it. Researchers in the field of artificial intelligence are in high demand.

A typical compensation for an AI researcher in the United States is $115,000 per year.

Artificial Intelligence Product Manager

Jobs for AI Product Managers tend to pay highly because of the responsibility involved in steering the development of an AI-based product or service. They work closely with engineers and data scientists to identify gaps in the market and plan for the introduction of innovative AI solutions. An AI Product Manager understands how to apply AI methods to any challenge, thanks to their familiarity with deep learning and machine learning. Using machine learning, they will be able to zero in on precisely what needs fixing in an existing product.

In the United States, an AI product manager can expect to earn an average annual salary of $120,000.

AI Consultant

An AI consultant offers advice to organizations on how they may integrate AI and machine learning into their workflow to boost productivity, cut expenses, and raise profits. They work together with engineers and other experts to help companies find ways to improve business processes by incorporating AI. It's a rather good paying field in the AI industry. In the United States, an AI consultant can expect to earn a median yearly salary of $120,000.

Martin kept staring at me interestingly while I roll out the list of these awesome career paths and he looked absolutely ready to jump in. and he was nodding his head in serious affirmation but I couldn't say which job fascinated him the most. He had made a comment that the data analysis seemed quite easy and the data consultant didn't sound like a lot of work. But when I told him that he needed a lot of mastery of data, artificial intelligence, digital and statistical skills as well as good knowledge of computer language, his head went and his enthusiasm disappeared.

"You are currently a secretary, you have worked with words and letters for a long time. If you are going to venture into AI you must get familiar with numbers and some more complex elements". I said to him, placing my hands on his shoulder to raise his spirit. But I know this young man, more than being lazy to work; he is also lazy to learn. But I had made a promise in my heart to motivate him and help him make it easy to get the scope. Mastering AI may sound like an impossible task to many; however, for anyone who is willing to have a good life in the future, there is need to understand the basics and essentials of this magical system from the world of aliens.

Part Two: Running Background Check on AI

A Sneak Peek into AI

AI is not as complex as it sounds but you must be willing to learn. Martin, my cousin, simply gave up some days into the training. I made him read some hefty books about statistics and syntax and he was like

"Why are you making this so difficult for me, can't you just tell me what I need to know?"

And then I said to him "No one can teach you to build the app you want to build, you need to learn yourself"

He looked at me with a firm smirk and dumped the book on my table. In the evening, I had thought up a good plan to get him to understand. So I called him and I was not going to put him through the basics but start from somewhere interesting.

For most people, the challenge is spending the time to understand the basics before jumping into practice. Although not everyone needs to learn AI to be able to use it, however the fundamental knowledge of the foundation of AI tools and models would make anyone who uses one two AI tools to be more familiar with what they are using. The field of Artificial Intelligence (AI) is majorly designed and projected to build and train machines to perform tasks that would otherwise require voluminous efforts and energy form human beings. Machine learning, deep learning, and operational rules are all sources of power for AI systems.

Due to its novelty, artificial intelligence (AI) presents both opportunities and dangers. It has the potential to improve efficiency and cut down on mistakes made by humans, but it also has the potential to make some jobs obsolete while spawning others. Although humanity have not yet been able to create self-aware AI devices, several scientists have raised alarm about their potential.

Computer vision, natural language processing, speech recognition, software engineering concepts, autonomous systems, machine learning, image analysis, signal and sound processing, ethics and societal implications of AI, etc. are just few of the many areas of study that fall under the umbrella of Artificial Intelligence. Working with AI requires an in-depth understanding of Math, Algorithms, Statistics, and Probability. Most people trained in artificial intelligence work for major tech firms, where they develop and improve software, hardware, and other systems. They design algorithms that help recommend shows and movies on sites like YouTube and Netflix, work to perfect the technology behind autonomous vehicles and unmanned aerial vehicles, and build helpful digital personal assistants. Also necessary is a deep understanding of computer programming languages. Graduates in the field of artificial intelligence can pursue careers as researchers, specialists, engineers in machine learning, computational linguistics, robotics, and other related fields. There is a wide range AI systems that are being developed and utilized in this field but we would only look at a few of them.

I said to Martin "how about we take a look at the make-up of these tools you are getting to like". He was no longer interested but he managed to drag himself to the interesting chat I had drawn on my board.

Chapter Five: Types of AI

Not all machines work the same and not all AI are programmed and designed the same way. You may love to see and read about the different dimensions of AI machines to see why each of them is unique in its own way. This would enable you understand them and know how best to use them.

Reactive Machines

Reactive machines are the simplest form of AI that don't have the ability to store past experiences or use past experiences to inform future decisions. They only react to the current situation based on pre-defined rules and can't form their own conclusions. They don't have the ability to learn and improve over time. These are the simplest, most primitive AI systems yet created. They mimic the way the human brain processes information in response to various inputs. The functionality of these machines does not rely on memory. Since they can't draw on past experiences to guide their current decisions, such robots can't be said to "learn." In other words, these devices could only be programmed to automatically react to a small number of inputs. They can't be made to rely on the same information stored in memory to perform better. Deep Blue, IBM's chess-playing artificial intelligence system that famously defeated Garry Kasparov in 1997, is a good example of a reactive AI machine. Examples of reactive machines include Deep Blue (IBM's chess-playing computer), AlphaGo (Google's computer program that defeated a world champion in the game of Go), Spam filters, Netflix recommendation engine and Chess-playing supercomputer.

Limited Memory

Limited memory AI systems have the ability to store past experiences to inform future decisions. They can access this past data to learn and improve performance over time. These types of AI are commonly used in self-driving cars and speech recognition systems. They are more advanced than reactive machines but still can't understand the context of the data they are processing. In addition to the capabilities of fully reactive machines, limited memory machines can also learn from past data and make judgments based on that knowledge. This branch of AI encompasses virtually every known use case. All modern AIs, including those that employ deep learning, are schooled by massive amounts of training data, which they memorize and use as a model to apply to new challenges.

For instance, hundreds of photos with labels are used to teach an AI how to identify items by scanning them and then labeling them. As it is given with new photos to analyze, this type of AI uses its previously acquired "learning experience" to more accurately attribute labels to those images. Today's chatbots, virtual assistants, and self-driving cars are all powered by limited memory AI.

Theory of Mind

Theory of Mind AI refers to the ability of an AI system to understand and predict human emotions, beliefs, and intentions. It requires a deep understanding of human psychology and involves the use of Natural Language Processing (NLP) and computer vision. Theory of Mind AI is still in the experimental stage, and researchers are trying to develop AI systems that can empathize with humans and communicate in a more human-like manner. Researchers are working to develop advanced AI systems, with theory of mind AI being the next step. Understanding the wants, feelings, beliefs, and mental processes of the people it interacts with is a key capability for a fully developed artificial intelligence. Achieving Theory of mind level AI will require growth in other fields of AI in addition to the burgeoning field of artificial emotional intelligence. This is because AI machines, in order to "understand" human needs, will have to view humans as unique individuals whose thoughts are susceptible to influence from a variety of sources.

Self-Aware

Self-aware AI systems are the most advanced form of AI. They not only have the ability to learn and improve over time but also have consciousness and self-awareness. They can understand their own existence, feelings, and emotions. Self-aware AI systems are still in the realm of science fiction, and researchers are trying to develop AI systems that can replicate human consciousness. This hypothetically-future stage of AI research is the pinnacle of the field. The term "self-aware AI" is quite self-explanatory; it refers to an artificial intelligence that has progressed to the point where it is mentally comparable to a human being. The end goal of all AI research has been and will always be the development of such an Ai, even though its realization is decades or even centuries away. In addition to being able to read and respond to human emotions, this AI will also be able to experience and express a wide range of feelings, wants, opinions, and even desires. This is the kind of artificial intelligence that worries technology pessimists. The advent of self-aware technology has the ability to greatly advance our civilization, but it also carries the risk of bringing about its demise. This is due to the fact that, once self-aware, the AI would be able to have thoughts like self-preservation, which might lead to the end of humanity in some way, since such an entity could easily outmaneuver the intellect of any human being and create sophisticated schemes to take over humanity. Artificial Narrow Intelligence (ANI), Artificial General Intelligence (AGI), and Artificial Superintelligence (ASI) constitute an alternative system of classification that is more commonly used in tech jargon.

Artificial Narrow Intelligence (ANI)

This sort of artificial intelligence encompasses all other forms of AI that are now in existence, including the most advanced and complex forms of AI that have ever been developed to this day. The term "artificial narrow intelligence" (AI) is used to describe AI systems that are only capable of carrying out a certain task independently by mimicking human capabilities. This means that these computers are only capable of carrying out the tasks that have been specifically designed for them, giving them a relatively restricted or narrow range of capabilities. These systems all fall under the reactive and limited memory AI category, according to the classification scheme that was just discussed. ANI encompasses even the most advanced forms of AI, such as those that gain new skills through a combination of machine learning and deep learning.

Artificial General Intelligence (AGI)

The capacity of an artificial intelligence agent to learn, observe, comprehend, and perform all human-like functions is the hallmark of artificial general intelligence (AGI). These systems will be capable of building various competences, making linkages and generalizations across domains, and doing so independently, which will drastically reduce the amount of time required for training. Because of this, AI systems will be able to replicate the multi-functional talents that people possess, making them just as capable as humans.

Artificial Superintelligence (ASI)

It is likely that the development of Artificial Superintelligence will signal the peak of AI research. This is because AGI will become by far the most capable forms of intelligence on earth once it has been developed. In addition to imitating the multifaceted intelligence of human humans, ASI will also be significantly superior at everything they do as a result of having a significantly larger memory, the ability to process and analyze data significantly more quickly, and the ability to make decisions significantly more quickly. The development of artificial general intelligence and augmented/synthetic intelligence will eventually result in a scenario that is most commonly known as the singularity. Even though the prospect of having such powerful machines at our disposal might seem tempting, there is a possibility that these machines could endanger either our very existence or, at the very least, our way of life.

But there is nothing to fear, we are humans and we always find our way around even the most difficult situations.

And here is my cousin, standing right beside me, staring at the board like a baby seeing a mirror for the first time. He looked confused and amazed at the same time.

"if only I could create one of these, I will make it sing lullabies to me in the bed, tell me what that hot secretary is wearing and reveal Andre's muscle secrets"

"Well" I replied, "it's not that difficult to build, you just need to go pack and pick the textbook you dropped on my table."

He laughed "I am never opening that book again bro".

"You don't have to tell me, I know. Here is the brief anyway."

Chapter Six: Foundations of AI

Remember the day you asked me what machine learning is. Well, I am in a good mood now and I care to explain. But first, you must promise to pay attention. These things need to be understood with interest.

Machine Learning

One of the very important aspects of AI is machine learning. Machine learning is the foundation of most systems developed on AI. Machine Learning (ML) is a subset of Artificial Intelligence (AI) that involves training computers to learn from data without being explicitly programmed. It is a process by which machines can learn and improve their performance on a task over time by analyzing and adapting to large amounts of data. The world we live in today is permeated by the processes of machine learning. When we engage with financial institutions, make purchases online, or use social media, machine learning algorithms are at work to ensure that our experiences are streamlined, trouble-free, and safe. We are only beginning to scratch the surface of machine learning's capabilities, despite the rapid development of both machine learning it and the technologies surrounding it.

Machine Learning algorithms can be broadly classified into three categories: Supervised Learning, Unsupervised Learning, and Reinforcement Learning.

Supervised Learning

Supervised Learning is the most commonly used type of Machine Learning. It involves training the machine to predict output values based on labeled input data. The labeled data is fed into the algorithm, and the machine learns to identify patterns in the data that are associated with the desired output. The algorithm then uses these patterns to make predictions on new, unlabeled data. Some common applications of supervised learning include image recognition, speech recognition, and natural language processing.

Unsupervised Learning

Unsupervised Learning is a type of Machine Learning that involves training the machine to identify patterns in unlabeled data. Unlike Supervised Learning, there is no labeled data to train the machine, so it must find patterns and relationships on its own. This makes Unsupervised Learning more challenging than Supervised Learning. Some common applications of Unsupervised

Learning include clustering, anomaly detection, and dimensionality reduction.

Reinforcement Learning

Reinforcement Learning is a type of Machine Learning that involves training the machine to make decisions based on feedback from the environment. In Reinforcement Learning, the machine is not given labeled data but instead must learn by trial and error. The machine interacts with the environment and receives rewards or penalties based on its actions. Over time, the machine learns which actions result in the highest rewards and adjusts its behavior accordingly. Reinforcement Learning is commonly used in robotics, game playing, and autonomous vehicles.

Machine Learning and Developers

In order to most effectively build models that learn over time using machine learning, developers will depend on their understanding of statistics, probability, and calculus when getting started. Developers shouldn't have any trouble picking up the tools that many other developers use to train current ML algorithms if they have strong expertise in these domains. Additionally, developers may choose whether or not their algorithms will be supervised.

106

Early on in a project, a developer may decide to make choices and build up a model. After that, the developer may step back and let the model learn on its own. The distinction between a developer and a data scientist is often hazy. Developers may sometimes combine data from a machine learning model, and data scientists will help create user-facing solutions. Collaboration between these two fields of study may increase the worth and use of ML initiatives.

Machine Learning and Business Goals

Although originally developed for online retailers, machine learning has found widespread use in many other sectors. In this strategy, companies use machine learning algorithms to identify, learn about, and keep their most profitable clients. In order to identify the highest-spending customers and the most devoted brand supporters, these value models analyze vast troves of consumer data. To estimate how much money a client will bring in over time, businesses might use customer lifetime value models. Having this knowledge allows businesses to direct their marketing efforts on boosting the frequency with which their most valuable clients engage with the brand. To attract new customers who are comparable to current high-value customers, businesses may use customer lifetime value models to better allocate their acquisition budgets.

It takes more effort and money to attract new clients than it does to maintain current ones happy and loyal. The purpose of customer churn modeling is to predict which consumers will cease using a service and why. An efficient churn model employs machine learning algorithms to provide information such as churn risk ratings for individual customers and the relative relevance of various churn sources. An algorithmic retention strategy relies heavily on these results. The best way for companies to retain their high-value consumers purchasing and coming back for more is to have a better understanding of customer turnover so they can improve discount offers, email campaigns, and other focused marketing activities.

Consumers can rapidly compare costs across many channels, and they have more options than ever before. Businesses may adapt to the ever-changing nature of the market with the help of dynamic pricing, also known as demand pricing. The amount of interest of the target consumer, the demand at the moment of purchase, and whether or not the buyer has participated with a marketing campaign are all elements that may influence the price at which an organization sells an item.

To be so nimble, a company needs a robust machine learning approach and a mountain of data on how consumers' willingness to pay for an item or service varies between contexts. Companies like airlines and ridesharing services have effectively utilized dynamic price optimization tactics to increase income, despite the complexity of dynamic pricing models.

Offering the right product to the right person at the right time has always been the key to effective marketing. Not very long ago, when it came to segmenting consumers into groups for focused ads, marketers depended on their own instincts. Data scientists may now utilize clustering and classification algorithms provided by machine learning to categorize clients into personas according to their unique characteristics. Each customer's demographics, browsing habits, and affinities are taken into account while creating these profiles. By associating these characteristics with buying habits, data-savvy businesses may launch targeted advertising efforts that are more likely to increase sales than broad-based ones.

The ability to tailor services to each individual customer's preferences will improve as firms have access to more data and as algorithmic sophistication rises.

It's not only the retail, finance, and e-commerce industries that can benefit from machine learning. The scientific, medical, building, and power uses for it are all quite promising as well. For instance, in image classification, machine learning algorithms are used to classify incoming images into one of a predefined set of categories. It may help with medical diagnosis, social media picture tagging, and modeling 3D building blueprints from 2D drawings.

Neural networks and other deep learning techniques are often employed for image classification because of their superior ability to detect important aspects of a picture in the presence of noise. They may compensate for problems like viewpoint, lighting, size, and clutter volume to provide the most relevant and high-quality insights possible.

Machine Learning Use Cases

Machine learning powers a variety of key business use cases. But how does it deliver competitive advantage? Among machine learning's most compelling qualities is its ability to automate and speed time to decision and accelerate time to value. That starts with gaining better business visibility and enhancing collaboration.

Traditionally what we see is people not being able to work together. Adding machine learning to Oracle Analytics Cloud ultimately helps people organize their work and build, train, and deploy these data models. It's a collaboration tool whose value is in accelerating the process and allowing different parts of the business to collaborate, giving you better quality and models for you to deploy.

For example, typical finance departments are routinely burdened by repeating a variance analysis process—a comparison between what is actual and what was forecast. It's a low-cognitive application that can benefit greatly from machine learning.

By embedding machine learning, finance can work faster and smarter, and pick up where the machine left off.

The power of Prediction

Another exciting capability of machine learning is its predictive capabilities. In the past, business decisions were often made based on historical outcomes. Today, machine learning employs rich analytics to predict what will happen. Organizations can make forward-looking, proactive decisions instead of relying on past data. For example, predictive maintenance can enable manufacturers, energy companies, and other industries to seize the initiative and ensure that their operations remain dependable and optimized. In an oil field with hundreds of drills in operation, machine learning models can spot equipment that's at risk of failure in the near future and then notify maintenance teams in advance. This approach not only maximizes productivity, it increases asset performance, uptime, and longevity. It can also minimize worker risk, decrease liability, and improve regulatory compliance. The benefits of predictive maintenance extend to inventory control and management. Avoiding unplanned equipment downtime by implementing predictive maintenance helps organizations more accurately predict the need for spare parts and repairs—significantly reducing capital and operating expenses.

Machine learning potential

Machine learning offers tremendous potential to help organizations derive business value from the wealth of data available today. However, inefficient workflows can hold companies back from realizing machine learning's maximum potential. To succeed at an enterprise level, machine learning needs to be part of a comprehensive platform that helps organizations simplify operations and deploy models at scale. The right solution will enable organizations to centralize all data science work in a collaborative platform and accelerate the use and management of open source tools, frameworks, and infrastructure.

Programming

Programming serves as one of the essential foundations of AI, enabling the development and implementation of intelligent systems and algorithms. It provides the means to instruct machines on how to perform specific tasks and make intelligent decisions. AI programming encompasses a range of languages and frameworks that facilitate the creation of AI models, algorithms, and applications.

One of the most prominent programming languages used in AI is Python. Python's simplicity, versatility, and vast library ecosystem make it a popular choice for AI development. Libraries such as NumPy, Pandas, and scikit-learn provide powerful tools for data manipulation, analysis, and machine learning. For instance, in natural language processing, Python-based libraries like NLTK and spaCy offer functionalities for text processing and analysis.

AI programming involves writing algorithms that mimic human cognitive abilities, such as learning, reasoning, and problem-solving. Machine learning algorithms, including supervised learning, unsupervised learning, and reinforcement learning, are implemented through programming to enable machines to learn from data and make predictions or take actions. For instance, in image classification, programmers design algorithms that process and analyze image data to identify objects or patterns, using techniques like convolutional neural networks (CNNs).

Moreover, AI programming is crucial for building intelligent agents and systems. These agents can interact with their environment, process sensory inputs, and make decisions based on learned patterns. For example, in autonomous driving, programmers write algorithms that enable a vehicle to analyze sensor data, such as cameras and LiDAR, to detect objects, plan routes, and control steering and acceleration.

Programming also plays a vital role in natural language processing and chatbots. Developers use programming languages to process and understand human language, perform sentiment analysis, and generate appropriate responses. AI-powered chatbots, like those used in customer service applications, utilize programming techniques to understand user queries, analyze intent, and provide relevant information or assistance.

Additionally, AI programming is essential for optimizing and fine-tuning AI models. Programmers utilize techniques like hyperparameter tuning, regularization, and cross-validation to improve the performance and generalization of machine learning models. They also implement techniques like ensemble learning, where multiple models are combined to make more accurate predictions, or deep learning architectures like recurrent neural networks (RNNs) for sequential data analysis.

Programming forms a foundational pillar of AI, enabling the development of intelligent systems, algorithms, and applications. Through programming, AI practitioners can design and implement machine learning algorithms, build intelligent agents, process and analyze data, create chatbots, and optimize AI models. The power of programming languages and frameworks, coupled with AI techniques, empowers developers to harness the potential of AI and drive innovation in various industries and   domains.

Programming Languages

Python

Python is a versatile and beginner-friendly programming language known for its simplicity and readability. It has gained immense popularity in the field of AI and data science due to its extensive library ecosystem. Python is widely used for tasks such as data manipulation, machine learning, web development, and automation. Libraries like NumPy, Pandas, and scikit-learn provide powerful tools for scientific computing, data analysis, and machine learning. For instance, TensorFlow and PyTorch, two popular deep learning frameworks, are extensively used in Python. Many AI-driven applications, including chatbots, recommendation systems, and image recognition systems, are built using Python.

Java

Java is a robust and widely adopted programming language with a strong focus on object-oriented programming. It is known for its platform independence, making it suitable for developing cross-platform applications. Java is commonly used for building enterprise-level applications, web development, and Android app development. Its scalability, security features, and rich ecosystem of libraries and frameworks make it a preferred choice for large-scale AI applications. Apache Mahout, a machine learning library, and Deeplearning4j, a deep learning library, are examples of Java-based tools used in AI. Additionally, Java's integration with Apache Hadoop and Apache Spark enables distributed processing of big data for AI applications.

R

R is a programming language specifically designed for statistical analysis and data visualization. It provides a wide range of statistical and graphical techniques, making it popular among statisticians and data scientists. R is commonly used for exploratory data analysis, statistical modeling, and machine learning. Its extensive collection of packages, such as caret and ggplot2, provide powerful tools for data manipulation, visualization, and predictive modeling. R is widely adopted in academia, healthcare research, and finance for data-driven decision-making. For example, the R language is used in bioinformatics for analyzing genomic data and in social sciences for conducting statistical analyses.

C++

C++ is a powerful and efficient programming language used in a variety of domains, including AI and game development. It offers low-level control, high performance, and a rich set of libraries. C++ is commonly used for developing AI algorithms, computer vision applications, and performance-critical systems. Libraries like OpenCV, which provides computer vision algorithms, and Eigen, which offers linear algebra operations, are widely used in AI projects. C++'s ability to interface with hardware and its efficient memory management make it suitable for applications that require real-time processing and performance optimization.

JavaScript

JavaScript is a versatile programming language primarily used for web development. It enables interactive and dynamic user interfaces, making it crucial for front-end web development. JavaScript has gained significance in AI through the rise of web-based AI applications and the development of libraries and frameworks like TensorFlow.js and Brain.js. These libraries allow developers to run machine learning models directly in the browser, opening up possibilities for AI-powered web applications. JavaScript's integration with HTML and CSS, along with its extensive browser support, make it a key language for building interactive AI-driven web experiences.

MATLAB

MATLAB is a high-level programming language designed for numerical computing and scientific research. It provides a comprehensive environment for algorithm development, data analysis, and visualization. MATLAB is commonly used in areas like signal processing, image and video processing, and control systems. It offers powerful toolboxes for machine learning, deep learning, and statistics. MATLAB's ease of use, extensive mathematical functions, and visualization capabilities make it a preferred choice for researchers and engineers working on AI applications in various domains.

Each programming language has its strengths and specific use cases within the realm of AI and beyond. Understanding the characteristics and applications of different programming languages empowers developers to choose the most suitable language for their AI projects, whether it's Python for its extensive libraries, Java for its scalability, R for statistical analysis, C++ for performance-critical tasks, JavaScript for web-based AI, or MATLAB for scientific research and numerical computing

Programming Paradigms

Programming paradigms refer to different approaches or styles of programming that guide the structure, organization, and flow of code. Each paradigm offers a distinct set of concepts, principles, and patterns to solve problems and design software. Let's explore some popular programming paradigms in detail:

Procedural Programming

Procedural programming is based on the idea of breaking down a program into smaller, reusable functions or procedures. It focuses on the sequential execution of instructions and emphasizes modularity and code reusability. In this paradigm, data and behavior are separated, and functions manipulate data through explicit parameters and return values. C and Pascal are examples of languages that follow the procedural paradigm. Procedural programming is well-suited for tasks that involve step-by-step procedures and algorithms.

Object-Oriented Programming (OOP)

Object-Oriented Programming revolves around the concept of objects, which combine data (attributes) and behavior (methods) into a single entity. It emphasizes the organization of code around objects that interact with each other through message passing. Encapsulation, inheritance, and polymorphism are key principles in OOP. Languages like Java, C++, and Python provide extensive support for OOP. OOP allows for better code organization, reusability, and modularity, making it suitable for large-scale projects and building complex systems.

Functional Programming

Functional Programming treats computation as the evaluation of mathematical functions and emphasizes immutability and the absence of side effects. It focuses on expressing computations as the composition of pure functions, where the output depends solely on the input. Functional programming languages such as Haskell, Lisp, and Scala provide strong support for this paradigm. Features like higher-order functions, recursion, and immutable data structures enable functional programming's elegance and conciseness. It excels in tasks related to data transformation, parallel computing, and concurrency.

Event-Driven Programming

Event-Driven Programming revolves around the handling of events, such as user actions or system notifications. It relies on event handlers or callbacks to respond to specific events. This paradigm is commonly used in graphical user interfaces (GUIs), web development, and real-time systems. Languages like JavaScript, which powers web browsers, heavily use event-driven programming. The asynchronous and non-blocking nature of event-driven programming allows for responsive and interactive applications.

Declarative Programming

Declarative Programming focuses on describing the desired outcome or result, rather than specifying the exact steps to achieve it. It allows programmers to define what needs to be done, and the underlying execution engine determines how to accomplish it. Two common types of declarative programming are:

Logic Programming

Logic programming languages like Prolog use rules and facts to express relationships and constraints. They are suitable for tasks involving search, inference, and symbolic reasoning.

SQL (Structured Query Language)

SQL is a declarative language used for querying and manipulating databases. It allows users to specify the desired data set without specifying how to retrieve it.

Understanding different programming paradigms enables developers to choose the most appropriate approach for specific tasks and project requirements. Some languages, like Python and Scala, support multiple paradigms, allowing flexibility and adaptability in designing software. The choice of paradigm depends on factors such as project complexity, team collaboration, performance requirements, and the problem domain. By embracing different paradigms, programmers can expand their problem-solving toolkit and develop more efficient, maintainable, and scalable software systems.

The future of programming holds immense potential and exciting possibilities. As technology continues to advance at a rapid pace, programming will play a crucial role in shaping our world. Let's delve into some key future trends in programming and explore the prospects they hold:

Artificial Intelligence (AI) and Machine Learning (ML)

AI and ML have already made a significant impact in various domains, and their influence will only grow stronger in the future. Programming will be pivotal in developing intelligent systems capable of learning, reasoning, and making decisions. As AI algorithms become more sophisticated, programmers will be at the forefront of creating innovative applications, such as autonomous vehicles, personalized medicine, smart assistants, and predictive analytics. The demand for AI and ML experts is skyrocketing, presenting exciting career opportunities for programmers with expertise in these domains.

Internet of Things (IoT)

The IoT is revolutionizing the way we interact with the physical world. It involves connecting everyday objects to the internet, enabling them to communicate and exchange data. Programming will be fundamental in designing and developing IoT devices, creating intelligent sensor networks, and managing the massive amounts of data generated by interconnected devices. As IoT adoption grows, programmers will have the chance to build smart homes, optimize industrial processes, develop wearable technology, and enhance healthcare systems through interconnected devices.

Augmented Reality (AR) and Virtual Reality (VR):

AR and VR technologies are rapidly evolving and opening up new realms of immersive experiences. These technologies rely heavily on programming to create virtual environments, simulate real-world scenarios, and provide interactive user interfaces. In the future, programmers will have opportunities to develop AR and VR applications in various domains, including gaming, education, architecture, healthcare, and training simulations. The fusion of AR/VR with AI and IoT will further amplify the potential of these technologies, creating transformative experiences and applications.

Quantum Computing

Quantum computing is poised to revolutionize computation by leveraging the principles of quantum mechanics. Although still in its early stages, quantum programming will become increasingly relevant as quantum computers become more accessible and powerful. Programming in this paradigm will require a deep understanding of quantum algorithms, quantum gates, and quantum data structures. Quantum programming has the potential to revolutionize fields like cryptography, optimization, drug discovery, and material science, solving complex problems that are currently computationally infeasible.

Automation and Robotics

Automation and robotics are reshaping industries and the workforce. Programming will be critical in developing intelligent robots, automation systems, and autonomous machines. Programmers will play a vital role in creating algorithms for robot perception, control, and decision-making. Industries such as manufacturing, healthcare, agriculture, logistics, and space exploration will rely on programming to optimize processes, increase efficiency, and enable human-robot collaboration. The demand for programmers skilled in robotics and automation will continue to rise.

The future prospects for programmers are promising. As technology continues to evolve, the demand for skilled programmers will remain high. Programmers who stay abreast of emerging technologies and acquire new skills will have exciting career opportunities in cutting-edge industries. The ability to adapt to new programming paradigms, languages, and frameworks will be crucial. Additionally, the interdisciplinary nature of programming will lead to collaboration with professionals from diverse fields, providing avenues for creativity and innovation.

Moreover, programming empowers individuals to transform their ideas into reality. It offers the ability to build solutions to pressing global challenges, drive innovation, and make a positive impact on society. The future of programming is not only about writing code but also about using technology as a force for good, addressing ethical considerations, and ensuring inclusivity and diversity in software development.

The future of programming holds limitless potential. With emerging technologies like AI, IoT, AR/VR, quantum computing, and automation, programmers have the opportunity to shape the future and make meaningful contributions to society. By embracing these trends, expanding skill sets, and fostering a passion for lifelong learning, programmers can embark on an exciting journey of exploration and innovation in the digital age.

Computer Vision

Computer vision is a crucial field within artificial intelligence (AI) that focuses on enabling computers to interpret and understand visual data, much like humans do. It plays a vital role in various applications, ranging from autonomous vehicles and surveillance systems to healthcare diagnostics and augmented reality. As a foundation of AI, computer vision encompasses several key subtopics, each contributing to the development of intelligent visual systems. Let's explore some of these subtopics and understand their significance in the realm of computer vision.

Image Classification

Image classification involves training algorithms to categorize images into specific classes or labels. This subtopic forms the basis of many computer vision applications, such as identifying objects in images or recognizing handwritten digits. Techniques like convolutional neural networks (CNNs) are widely used to extract meaningful features from images and make accurate predictions.

Object Detection

Object detection aims to identify and locate multiple objects within an image or a video stream. This subtopic is essential for tasks like autonomous driving, where detecting and tracking pedestrians, vehicles, and traffic signs are crucial. Advanced algorithms, such as the region-based convolutional neural network (R-CNN) and its variants, have revolutionized object detection by combining localization and classification.

Semantic Segmentation

Semantic segmentation involves dividing an image into different regions and assigning each pixel a specific label, providing a detailed understanding of the scene's structure. This subtopic finds applications in medical imaging, autonomous robotics, and video surveillance. Techniques like the fully convolutional network (FCN) and U-Net have significantly advanced semantic segmentation capabilities.

Object Tracking

Object tracking focuses on following and monitoring the movement of specific objects across consecutive frames in a video. It is crucial for tasks like surveillance, video analysis, and human-computer interaction. Various approaches, such as correlation filters and deep learning-based trackers, have been developed to improve object tracking accuracy and robustness.

Image Generation

Image generation involves creating new images based on learned patterns and styles. This subtopic has gained significant attention with the advent of generative adversarial networks (GANs) and their ability to generate realistic images, such as faces, landscapes, and artwork. Image generation finds applications in creative fields, data augmentation, and simulations.

3D Reconstruction

3D reconstruction aims to create a three-dimensional representation of a scene or an object from multiple 2D images or video frames. This subtopic finds applications in fields like architecture, virtual reality, and autonomous navigation. Techniques like structure from motion (SfM) and simultaneous localization and mapping (SLAM) enable accurate 3D reconstructions from visual data.

Visual Understanding and Reasoning

Visual understanding and reasoning involve higher-level interpretation of visual data, such as inferring relationships, answering questions, and understanding context. This subtopic combines computer vision with natural language processing and knowledge representation to enable AI systems to comprehend visual information and engage in more sophisticated tasks.

Techniques and Tools in Computer Vision

Computer vision, as a field within artificial intelligence, relies on a range of techniques and tools to analyze and interpret visual data. These techniques and tools play a crucial role in enabling machines to perceive and understand the visual world, leading to advancements in applications like object detection, image segmentation, and image recognition. Let's explore some of the key techniques and tools used in computer vision.

Convolutional Neural Networks (CNNs)

CNNs are deep learning models specifically designed for processing visual data. They consist of multiple layers of interconnected neurons that perform operations like convolution, pooling, and nonlinear activation. CNNs excel at feature extraction, allowing them to automatically learn and identify patterns, shapes, and textures in images. They have revolutionized computer vision tasks like image classification, object detection, and semantic segmentation.

Transfer Learning

Transfer learning is a technique that leverages pre-trained models to solve new visual tasks with limited labeled data. Instead of training a model from scratch, transfer learning involves using the knowledge learned by a model on a large dataset (e.g., ImageNet) and applying it to a different but related task. This approach saves computational resources and accelerates the development of computer vision applications.

Image Augmentation

Image augmentation techniques involve applying various transformations to existing images to create additional training data. By augmenting the dataset with variations like rotations, translations, scaling, and flipping, models become more robust and can generalize better to unseen data. Image augmentation helps overcome limitations posed by limited training data and improves the overall performance of computer vision models.

OpenCV

OpenCV (Open Source Computer Vision Library) is a popular open-source library that provides a wide range of computer vision algorithms and tools. It supports various programming languages like Python, C++, and Java and offers functionalities for image and video processing, feature detection, object tracking, and camera calibration. OpenCV serves as a versatile and accessible resource for implementing computer vision applications.

DeepLab

DeepLab is a state-of-the-art semantic image segmentation algorithm. It utilizes a deep convolutional neural network architecture coupled with atrous (dilated) convolutions to capture fine-grained details while maintaining a large receptive field. DeepLab has achieved impressive results in accurately segmenting objects within images and is widely used in applications like medical imaging, autonomous driving, and video surveillance.

YOLO (You Only Look Once)

YOLO is an object detection algorithm known for its real-time performance. Unlike traditional object detection algorithms that use region proposal techniques,

133

YOLO frames object detection as a regression problem, predicting bounding boxes and class probabilities directly from the entire image in a single pass. YOLO has gained popularity for its speed and accuracy, making it suitable for real-time applications like video analysis and robotics.

TensorFlow and PyTorch

TensorFlow and PyTorch are two popular deep learning frameworks used extensively in computer vision research and development. These frameworks provide a wide range of tools, pre-trained models, and APIs that facilitate the implementation of computer vision algorithms. They offer support for neural network construction, optimization, and deployment, empowering researchers and developers to build sophisticated computer vision systems.

GPU Computing

Graphics Processing Units (GPUs) are powerful hardware accelerators that significantly speed up computations in computer vision. With their parallel processing capabilities, GPUs enable efficient training and inference of deep learning models, reducing the time required for complex computer vision tasks. Frameworks like CUDA from NVIDIA provide programming interfaces for GPU computing, making it accessible to developers.

These techniques and tools have paved the way for significant advancements in computer vision, allowing machines to perform complex visual tasks with accuracy and efficiency. From image classification and object detection to semantic segmentation and real-time analysis, computer vision techniques and tools are instrumental in unlocking the potential of visual data and driving innovation in various industries.

The advancements in computer vision have been fueled by the availability of large-scale annotated datasets, powerful computational resources, and deep learning techniques. Deep neural networks, particularly convolutional neural networks, have revolutionized computer vision by enabling hierarchical feature extraction and end-to-end learning. Additionally, the availability of pre-trained models and frameworks, such as TensorFlow and PyTorch, has simplified the development and deployment of computer vision applications.

The practical implications of computer vision are vast and wide-ranging. In autonomous vehicles, computer vision systems analyze sensor data to detect and track objects, read traffic signs, and navigate complex road scenarios. In healthcare, computer vision assists in medical imaging analysis, disease diagnosis, and surgical procedures. In retail, computer vision powers object recognition for inventory management and personalized shopping experiences. These are just a few examples highlighting the transformative impact of computer vision across industries.

As computer vision continues to advance, the integration of other AI disciplines, such as natural language processing and reinforcement learning, will further enhance its capabilities. The combination of computer vision with other AI techniques opens up possibilities for more intelligent and interactive systems that can perceive and understand the visual world, enabling machines to interact with humans in a more natural and intuitive manner.

Computer vision serves as a foundation of AI by enabling machines to interpret and understand visual data. Its subtopics, including image classification, object detection, semantic segmentation, object tracking, image generation, 3D reconstruction, and visual understanding, contribute to the development of intelligent visual systems. With the continuous progress in algorithms, datasets, and computational resources, computer vision is revolutionizing industries and shaping the future of AI.

Chapter Seven: AI Tools and Use Cases

Let's take a work through awesome AI tools and their use cases.

Having background knowledge of AI tools and their use cases is becoming increasingly important in today's technology-driven world. AI is transforming industries and shaping the future of various domains, including healthcare, finance, marketing, and more. Understanding AI tools and their applications allows individuals to stay updated with the latest advancements and leverage the power of AI in their respective fields. It enables professionals to identify opportunities where AI can enhance efficiency, productivity, and decision-making processes. By familiarizing themselves with AI tools and their use cases, people can unlock new possibilities, solve complex problems, and drive innovation in their work. Whether you're a software developer, data scientist, business analyst, or a professional in any other field, having a solid understanding of AI tools equips you with a competitive edge and opens doors to exciting opportunities. So, dive into the world of AI tools, explore their potential, and empower yourself to be at the forefront of technological advancements!

OpenAI GPT-3

OpenAI's GPT-3 (Generative Pre-trained Transformer 3) is a groundbreaking language model that has revolutionized the field of natural language processing. It can understand and generate human-like text, enabling a wide range of applications. GPT-3 is used for language translation, content generation, chatbots, virtual assistants, and much more. Companies like OpenAI itself, as well as organizations like chatbot platform ChatGPT and content generation tool Copy.ai, rely on GPT-3's capabilities. GPT-3's impressive language understanding and generation capabilities make it a powerful tool for anyone looking to leverage advanced natural language processing in their applications.

TensorFlow

Developed by Google, TensorFlow is an open-source machine learning framework that has become immensely popular for building and deploying machine learning models. It provides a comprehensive ecosystem of tools and resources for training and deploying models across various domains. TensorFlow's versatility allows it to be used for a wide range of applications, such as image and speech recognition, natural language processing, recommendation systems, and more. Major companies like Airbnb, Intel, and Snapchat have adopted TensorFlow for their machine learning needs, utilizing its powerful capabilities and extensive community support.

PyTorch

PyTorch is another widely-used open-source machine learning framework known for its flexibility and user-friendly interface. It offers dynamic computational graphs, making it ideal for research and experimentation. PyTorch has gained popularity among researchers and practitioners in fields such as computer vision, natural language processing, and deep reinforcement learning. Companies like Facebook, Twitter, and Salesforce have utilized PyTorch for various AI projects. Its ease of use, extensive library support, and efficient execution make it a popular choice for building and training neural networks.

Hugging Face Transformers

Hugging Face Transformers is a Python library that provides pre-trained models and utilities for natural language processing tasks. It simplifies the development and deployment of models for tasks such as sentiment analysis, named entity recognition, question answering, and text generation. Companies like Airbnb, Bloomberg, and Microsoft have adopted Hugging Face Transformers for their NLP needs. The library's wide range of pre-trained models, easy-to-use API, and active community make it a go-to choice for NLP practitioners and researchers.

NVIDIA CUDA

NVIDIA CUDA is a parallel computing platform and API that allows developers to harness the power of NVIDIA GPUs for accelerated AI and deep learning computations. It enables the efficient utilization of GPU resources, significantly speeding up training and inference processes for machine learning models. Many companies and researchers, such as Adobe, BMW, and Stanford University, utilize NVIDIA CUDA for computationally intensive AI tasks. CUDA's ability to leverage GPU parallelism and its widespread adoption in the AI community make it a key tool for high-performance computing and deep learning.

IBM Watson

IBM Watson is a comprehensive suite of AI services and tools offered by IBM. It provides a range of capabilities, including natural language understanding, speech recognition, computer vision, and more. Watson's services enable companies to develop AI-powered applications for tasks like sentiment analysis, language translation, and customer support automation. Prominent organizations like H&R Block, Sesame Street, and UBS rely on IBM Watson for their AI-driven solutions. IBM Watson's broad functionality and enterprise-grade offerings make it a trusted choice for companies seeking to integrate advanced AI capabilities into their workflows.

Microsoft Azure Cognitive Services

Microsoft Azure Cognitive Services is a collection of AI services provided by Microsoft. It offers pre-built APIs and SDKs for tasks such as text analytics, image recognition, speech-to-text conversion, and more. Azure Cognitive Services enable developers to easily integrate AI capabilities into their applications without requiring extensive AI expertise. Companies like Coca-Cola, Uber, and HP have leveraged Azure Cognitive Services to enhance their products and services with AI capabilities. The broad range of AI services, seamless integration with Azure cloud infrastructure, and the extensive Microsoft ecosystem make Azure Cognitive Services a popular choice for AI development.

Google Cloud AI Platform

Google Cloud AI Platform provides a comprehensive set of tools and services for building, training, and deploying machine learning models on Google Cloud. It offers features like AutoML for automating the model development process, AI Platform Notebooks for collaborative coding environments, and AI Platform Pipelines for building end-to-end machine learning workflows. Major companies like Spotify, Airbus, and PayPal utilize Google Cloud AI Platform for their AI initiatives. Its robust infrastructure, scalability, and integration with other Google Cloud services make it a preferred platform for AI development and deployment.

Amazon AWS AI Services

Amazon Web Services (AWS) offers a range of AI services that provide pre-built capabilities for image recognition, natural language processing, speech analysis, and more. AWS AI Services, such as Amazon Rekognition, Amazon Comprehend, and Amazon Polly, enable developers to easily incorporate AI functionalities into their applications. Companies like Netflix, Airbnb, and Pinterest have leveraged AWS AI Services to enhance their user experiences and drive innovation. AWS's extensive suite of services, scalability, and integration with other AWS offerings make it a popular choice for AI development and deployment.

RapidAPI

RapidAPI is a platform that allows developers to discover, test, and integrate APIs from various AI providers. It provides a centralized interface for accessing and utilizing AI functionalities from different sources. RapidAPI offers a wide range of AI-related APIs, including language translation, sentiment analysis, facial recognition, and more. Developers and companies like Cisco, Deloitte, and Hyundai leverage RapidAPI to access AI capabilities without the need to develop them from scratch. RapidAPI's extensive API marketplace, ease of integration, and streamlined API management make it a valuable tool for developers seeking to incorporate AI functionalities into their applications.

You Can Try The Magic Words: Try Building Your Own Model

Well, you probably still have to do an in-depth research but I am sure I have pointed you to the direction of your adventure. After selecting an AI tool to use, you can start making attempts at creating your own model. But I can assure you, you won't get it with the first trial. But you would get it with consistency and hard work.

Part Three: Welcome to the Future

Chapter Eight: Unlearning and Learning

For most of us, we know too much and that vast volume of knowledge is more a load than a value. For Martin, it's all about instructions, what to do and what to put in place for the next meeting, for the conference or for the next big customer at the sock company. However, the workplace is changing, even the customers now no longer come themselves, the meetings are being held on zoom and the workplace is less paper and more metal. That was the birth of his dilemma but he is almost over it now.

In today's rapidly evolving technological landscape, understanding AI is becoming increasingly crucial for individuals to thrive in the modern workplace. Those who lack knowledge and awareness of AI face several challenges that can hinder their ability to adapt and succeed in automated environments. Firstly, without understanding AI, individuals may struggle to comprehend and leverage the benefits of automation. AI-driven systems can streamline processes, increase efficiency, and handle repetitive tasks, enabling organizations to operate at a higher level. However, those who lack AI literacy may find themselves overwhelmed by these technologies, unable to take advantage of their potential. Secondly, the lack of AI understanding may hinder individuals' ability to effectively collaborate with intelligent machines. In many workplaces, human-machine interaction is becoming more prevalent, with AI systems assisting with decision-making, data analysis, and customer interactions. Without a foundational understanding of AI, individuals may struggle to work alongside these systems, leading to inefficient workflows and missed opportunities. Furthermore, the inability to adapt to AI-driven tools and technologies can limit career prospects. Many industries are embracing AI solutions, and job roles are evolving to require a basic understanding of AI concepts and applications. Individuals who fail to keep pace with these changes may find themselves at a disadvantage when seeking employment or career advancement opportunities.

Lastly, the lack of AI knowledge can also result in the perpetuation of biases and ethical concerns. AI algorithms are not infallible, and without an understanding of their limitations and potential biases, individuals may unknowingly perpetuate discriminatory practices or make decisions based on flawed insights. This can have serious consequences, both for individuals and the organizations they work for. Therefore, it is imperative for individuals to invest in AI education and upskilling to navigate the modern automated workplace successfully. By embracing AI literacy, individuals can position themselves to harness the potential of AI, collaborate effectively with intelligent systems, adapt to changing job requirements, and address ethical considerations in the AI-powered world.

Unlearning

Unlearning is an essential process for individuals seeking to understand AI and thrive in the modern automated workplace. In a rapidly evolving technological landscape, where AI is reshaping industries and transforming job roles, it is crucial to let go of outdated notions and embrace new knowledge and skills. Unlearning involves challenging preconceived ideas, questioning traditional practices, and being open to relearning and adapting to new ways of thinking and working.

To comprehend AI and its implications fully, one must be willing to shed any misconceptions or fears associated with the technology. AI is often portrayed in popular culture as a force that will replace human workers or bring about the downfall of society. While it is true that AI can automate certain tasks, it is important to recognize that it also brings numerous opportunities for innovation, efficiency, and new job roles. Unlearning involves letting go of these preconceived notions and approaching AI with an open mind, ready to explore its potential applications and benefits.

Unlearning also requires individuals to challenge the notion that AI is a mysterious and unattainable field reserved for experts and data scientists. While there are specialized roles within the AI domain, understanding the basics of AI is within reach for individuals from various backgrounds. Unlearning the belief that AI is only for technical experts enables individuals to engage with AI concepts and technologies, empowering them to contribute their unique perspectives and skills to the AI-driven workplace.

Furthermore, unlearning involves questioning traditional work practices that may be inefficient or redundant in the context of AI. As AI systems take over repetitive and mundane tasks, individuals have the opportunity to focus on higher-level cognitive activities that require creativity, critical thinking, and emotional intelligence. Unlearning the reliance on outdated work practices and embracing the possibilities offered by AI enables individuals to reevaluate their roles, explore new avenues of contribution, and redefine their professional identities.

Unlearning is not just about acquiring new knowledge but also about developing new skills that are relevant in the AI-driven workplace. With automation and AI becoming integral parts of many job roles, individuals need to adapt and acquire skills that complement AI systems. This includes skills such as data literacy, understanding AI algorithms, and being proficient in working with AI tools and platforms. Unlearning involves recognizing the gaps in one's skill set and actively seeking opportunities to upskill and reskill in order to remain relevant and competitive in the evolving job market.

Additionally, unlearning enables individuals to navigate the ethical considerations associated with AI. As AI systems become more powerful and influential, questions of bias, privacy, and accountability come to the forefront. Unlearning involves understanding the ethical implications of AI and critically examining the algorithms and data used in AI systems. It requires individuals to question the potential biases embedded in AI models and actively work towards developing fair and transparent AI solutions. Unlearning the assumption that AI is infallible and unbiased allows individuals to take a proactive approach in addressing ethical concerns and ensuring that AI technologies are developed and deployed responsibly.

Unlearning is a continuous process, as the field of AI continues to advance and evolve. Staying updated with the latest developments, trends, and best practices is essential for individuals looking to navigate the AI-driven workplace successfully. Engaging in continuous learning opportunities, such as online courses, workshops, and industry conferences, helps individuals keep pace with the rapidly changing landscape of AI. Unlearning becomes a lifelong journey of growth and adaptation, allowing individuals to continually evolve their understanding of AI and apply that knowledge effectively in their professional lives.

In conclusion, unlearning is a crucial process for individuals seeking to understand AI and thrive in the modern automated workplace. By letting go of outdated notions, questioning traditional practices, and embracing new knowledge and skills, individuals can adapt and evolve in the face of AI-driven transformations. Unlearning enables individuals to approach AI with an open mind, explore its potential applications, and contribute their unique perspectives and skills to the AI-driven workplace. It empowers individuals to reevaluate their roles, acquire relevant skills, navigate ethical considerations, and stay updated with the latest advancements in the field. Embracing unlearning as a continuous process allows individuals to harness the potential of AI, remain adaptable in the face of change, and shape the future of work in the AI-driven era.

Learning

Learning is the cornerstone for individuals seeking to understand AI and thrive in the modern automated workplace. In a world shaped by rapid technological advancements, embracing a continuous learning mindset is crucial to keep pace with the transformative power of AI. By actively engaging in learning endeavors, individuals can gain the knowledge and skills needed to comprehend AI, adapt to changing work dynamics, and unlock new opportunities for personal and professional growth.

To understand AI, one must embark on a learning journey that starts with grasping the foundational concepts. This includes acquiring knowledge about machine learning, neural networks, data analysis, and other key components of AI. Learning the basics of AI provides individuals with a solid framework to comprehend its capabilities, limitations, and potential applications. It allows them to navigate the AI landscape with confidence and understand the terminology and concepts that shape discussions around AI technologies.

Moreover, learning about AI enables individuals to appreciate its impact on various industries and job roles. AI is revolutionizing fields such as healthcare, finance, manufacturing, and customer service, among others. By actively seeking knowledge about AI's implications in specific domains, individuals can identify opportunities for applying AI solutions in their own work or explore new career paths. Understanding the potential of AI in different industries empowers individuals to evolve and adapt in an ever-changing job market.

Learning about AI also involves gaining practical skills to effectively work with AI technologies and tools. This includes developing proficiency in programming languages commonly used in AI, such as Python, R, or Java, and learning to leverage AI frameworks and libraries like TensorFlow or PyTorch. By acquiring hands-on experience with AI tools, individuals can explore data analysis, model building, and evaluation techniques.

Practical learning experiences not only enhance understanding but also build the confidence to apply AI in real-world scenarios.

Additionally, learning about AI ethics and responsible AI practices is crucial in the modern automated workplace. As AI becomes more pervasive, individuals need to develop a deep understanding of the ethical implications of AI systems. Learning about bias, fairness, transparency, and accountability in AI enables individuals to navigate the ethical challenges that arise with AI technologies. By staying informed and actively engaging in discussions around AI ethics, individuals can contribute to the development and adoption of responsible AI practices.

In the modern automated workplace, continuous learning is vital for individuals to cope with the ever-evolving AI landscape. As AI technologies advance and new applications emerge, individuals must stay updated with the latest developments. This requires a commitment to lifelong learning and a willingness to explore new avenues of knowledge. Engaging in online courses, attending workshops, participating in industry conferences, and joining AI communities are effective ways to stay abreast of AI advancements. By actively seeking out learning opportunities, individuals can stay relevant and adaptable in a world driven by AI.

Furthermore, learning fosters a growth mindset, which is essential for individuals to embrace the challenges and opportunities presented by AI. A growth mindset involves seeing failures and setbacks as learning opportunities, being open to feedback, and persisting in the face of challenges. The journey of learning about AI may involve encountering complex algorithms, technical hurdles, and conceptual difficulties. However, with a growth mindset, individuals can approach these challenges with enthusiasm and determination, knowing that each obstacle presents an opportunity for growth and improvement.

In the context of the modern automated workplace, learning AI-related skills also enhances job prospects and career growth. Employers are increasingly seeking professionals with AI knowledge and expertise. By demonstrating a commitment to learning and showcasing proficiency in AI technologies, individuals can differentiate themselves in the job market. Furthermore, continuous learning in AI allows individuals to adapt to changing job requirements and take advantage of new opportunities that arise as AI becomes more integrated into various industries.

Lastly, learning about AI fosters a sense of empowerment and agency. Instead of being passive recipients of AI-driven changes, individuals who invest in learning take an active role in shaping their future. They can participate in AI projects, contribute innovative ideas, and drive positive change within their organizations. Learning about AI equips individuals with the knowledge and skills to collaborate effectively with intelligent machines, leveraging their capabilities to augment human work and achieve greater productivity and efficiency.

Learning is essential for individuals seeking to understand AI and excel in the modern automated workplace. By embracing a continuous learning mindset, individuals can acquire the knowledge, skills, and ethical understanding needed to comprehend AI technologies, adapt to changing work dynamics, and harness the potential of AI for personal and professional growth. Learning empowers individuals to navigate the AI landscape confidently, explore new opportunities, stay relevant in a rapidly evolving job market, and contribute to the responsible and ethical development of AI technologies.

There are various mediums available for individuals to learn about utilizing AI for work and in the automated workplace. These mediums provide opportunities to acquire knowledge, develop skills, and gain practical experience in AI applications. Let's explore some of the common mediums of learning in this domain:

Online Courses and Tutorials

Online platforms like Coursera, Udemy, and edX offer a wide range of courses on AI, machine learning, and related topics. These courses provide structured learning materials, video lectures, and hands-on exercises to help individuals understand AI concepts and apply them in practical scenarios. Tutorials and video series on platforms like YouTube also offer valuable resources for learning AI techniques and tools.

AI Specialization Programs

Many universities and educational institutions offer specialized programs in AI, such as master's degrees or graduate certificates. These programs delve deeper into AI theory, algorithms, and applications, providing a comprehensive understanding of the subject. Enrolling in such programs allows individuals to gain in-depth knowledge and expertise in AI and its use in the workplace.

AI Bootcamps

AI bootcamps provide intensive and immersive learning experiences focused on practical applications of AI. These short-term programs often include hands-on projects, real-world case studies, and mentorship from industry professionals. Bootcamps offer an accelerated learning environment, enabling individuals to quickly gain AI skills and develop practical solutions for the workplace.

Industry Conferences and Workshops

Attending conferences and workshops focused on AI and automation provides opportunities to learn from experts in the field, network with industry professionals, and stay updated with the latest trends and advancements. These events often feature keynote speeches, panel discussions, and interactive sessions where participants can learn about best practices, real-world use cases, and emerging technologies in the AI domain.

Online AI Communities and Forums

Engaging with online AI communities and forums, such as Kaggle, AI Stack Exchange, and AI-related subreddits, allows individuals to connect with like-minded individuals, ask questions, share knowledge, and collaborate on AI projects. These communities provide a platform for learning from experienced practitioners, discussing AI challenges, and staying informed about the latest developments in the field.

AI Research Papers and Publications

Reading research papers and publications in the field of AI enables individuals to gain insights into cutting-edge algorithms, techniques, and advancements. Platforms like ArXiv, IEEE Xplore, and Google Scholar provide access to a vast repository of AI-related research papers. Exploring academic papers helps individuals understand the theoretical foundations of AI and keeps them abreast of the latest research findings.

Collaborative Projects and Hackathons

Participating in collaborative AI projects or hackathons allows individuals to work on real-world problems, collaborate with peers, and apply AI techniques in practical settings. These hands-on experiences provide valuable learning opportunities and foster a deeper understanding of AI concepts and their applications in the workplace.

In-house Training and Workshops

Many organizations offer in-house training programs and workshops to upskill their workforce in AI technologies and applications. These initiatives provide employees with the knowledge and skills necessary to leverage AI tools and contribute to AI-driven projects within their organizations.

AI Tool and Platform Documentation

AI tools and platforms, such as TensorFlow, PyTorch, and Azure AI, often provide comprehensive documentation and tutorials. Exploring the official documentation of these tools helps individuals understand their functionalities, best practices, and integration methods. It enables individuals to learn by experimenting with the tools and applying them to real-world scenarios.

Collaborating with AI Professionals

Working alongside AI professionals, either within the organization or through mentorship programs, provides valuable learning opportunities. Collaborating with experts in the field allows individuals to gain insights into practical AI applications, learn from their experiences, and receive guidance on utilizing AI effectively in the workplace.

Individuals have a wide array of mediums available to learn about utilizing AI for work and in the automated workplace. Online courses, specialized programs, bootcamps, conferences, online communities, research papers, collaborative projects, in-house training, and collaborations with AI professionals all offer avenues for individuals to acquire knowledge, develop skills, and gain practical experience in AI applications. By leveraging these mediums, individuals can enhance their understanding of AI, adapt to the automated workplace, and contribute to the advancement of AI-driven initiatives

Tracking the Updates

In today's fast-paced world, keeping up with industrial, technological, niche, and business trends is crucial for better understanding and utility of AI, as well as for staying updated and relevant in the modern automated workplace. With rapid advancements in technology and evolving business landscapes, individuals who stay informed about the latest trends are better equipped to harness the power of AI, make informed decisions, and adapt to the changing dynamics of their industries.

Industrial trends encompass the macro-level shifts and developments occurring within specific sectors or industries. By staying attuned to these trends, individuals can understand how AI is being applied in their respective fields and identify opportunities for its implementation. For instance, in healthcare, the trend of AI-enabled diagnostics and personalized medicine is revolutionizing patient care. By staying updated on these trends, medical professionals can leverage AI tools to analyze complex data and make more accurate diagnoses, ultimately improving patient outcomes.

Technological trends are key drivers of AI advancements and are essential for individuals seeking to understand and utilize AI effectively. These trends encompass breakthroughs in AI algorithms, advancements in hardware infrastructure, and the emergence of new AI tools and frameworks. Staying abreast of technological trends allows individuals to explore cutting-edge AI techniques, adopt more efficient AI solutions, and optimize their workflow. For example, the rise of deep learning and the availability of powerful GPU hardware have paved the way for significant advancements in natural language processing, computer vision, and speech recognition.

Niche trends refer to the specific areas or subfields within AI that are experiencing notable developments and growth. These trends often emerge from interdisciplinary collaborations and specialized research efforts. By keeping up with niche trends, individuals can gain insights into the latest research findings, innovative applications, and emerging techniques within their areas of interest. For instance, the niche trend of Explainable AI (XAI) focuses on developing AI models and algorithms that provide transparent explanations for their decisions. Understanding this trend enables individuals to design AI systems that are more interpretable and trustworthy.

Business trends are vital for individuals seeking to integrate AI into their organizations and maximize its impact. These trends encompass the adoption of AI by companies, the emergence of AI-driven business models, and the evolving customer expectations in an AI-driven marketplace. By following business trends, individuals can identify potential AI use cases, understand the competitive landscape, and make informed decisions regarding AI implementation strategies. For example, the trend of AI-powered chatbots in customer service has enabled companies to provide personalized and efficient support, enhancing customer satisfaction and loyalty.

To keep up with these diverse trends, individuals can adopt various strategies and approaches:

Continuous Learning

Engage in continuous learning by participating in online courses, attending workshops, and joining professional communities. These learning opportunities provide insights into the latest trends, industry best practices, and emerging technologies.

Industry Publications and News

Follow industry-specific publications, journals, and newsletters to stay updated on industrial and niche trends. These sources often feature articles, case studies, and expert opinions that shed light on the latest AI applications and advancements in specific sectors.

Technology Conferences and Events

Attend technology conferences and industry events focused on AI and related fields. These gatherings provide a platform to network with professionals, listen to keynote speeches, and participate in discussions on the latest trends and advancements.

Thought Leaders and Influencers

Follow thought leaders and influencers in the AI community through blogs, social media, and podcasts. These individuals often share valuable insights, discuss emerging trends, and provide thought-provoking perspectives on the future of AI.

Collaborative Projects and Partnerships

Engage in collaborative projects and partnerships with organizations and professionals who are at the forefront of AI developments. These collaborations offer opportunities to learn from industry leaders, gain exposure to innovative AI applications, and stay updated on the latest trends.

Industry Associations and Professional Networks

Join industry associations and professional networks relevant to your field. These organizations often organize events, webinars, and networking opportunities that facilitate knowledge sharing and keep members informed about industry trends and advancements.

Market Research and Competitive Analysis

Conduct market research and competitive analysis to understand how AI is being adopted and leveraged by competitors and industry leaders. This information helps individuals identify gaps, explore new opportunities, and develop strategies to stay ahead in the AI-driven marketplace.

Collaboration with AI Specialist

Collaborate with AI specialists, data scientists, and experts in the field to gain insights into the latest AI trends and applications. By working together, individuals can gain practical knowledge, exchange ideas, and leverage the expertise of AI professionals.

By actively keeping up with industrial, technological, niche, and business trends, individuals can gain a comprehensive understanding of AI's applications and implications. This knowledge allows them to make informed decisions, adapt to the changing workplace, and unlock the full potential of AI to drive innovation and growth. It positions individuals as valuable assets within their organizations and ensures their relevance in the modern automated workplace. Embracing these trends empowers individuals to contribute meaningfully to AI-driven initiatives, shape the future of their industries, and create a positive impact in an increasingly AI-centric world.

Chapter Nine: Embracing the Gig Economy

The gig economy, characterized by short-term contracts and freelance work, has gained significant traction in recent years, offering individuals new prospects for work and income generation. With the rise of AI and automation, the gig economy presents a promising avenue to leverage technology and avoid job loss. In this era of rapid technological advancements, traditional job roles are being reshaped, and new job types are emerging, driven by the integration of AI into various industries.

Let's explore the gig economy and some of the job types that hold future prospects in utilizing AI. The gig economy has reshaped the traditional employment landscape, offering individuals the opportunity to engage in short-term, flexible work arrangements. It encompasses a wide range of jobs across different industries, each with its own scope and benefits. Let's explore some popular job categories within the gig economy and the advantages they bring.

Freelance Writing and Content Creation

Freelance writers and content creators are in high demand as businesses seek quality content for their websites, blogs, and marketing materials. Freelancers have the freedom to choose their clients and projects, allowing them to showcase their writing skills and build a diverse portfolio. They can work with multiple clients simultaneously, expanding their network and gaining expertise in various industries. The gig nature of this work allows writers to have flexibility in their schedules and the potential for higher earning potential.

Graphic Design and Creative Services

With the increasing need for visually appealing content, graphic designers and creative professionals have ample opportunities in the gig economy. They can work on a project-by-project basis, designing logos, websites, marketing materials, and more. Freelancers in this field have the creative freedom to explore diverse projects, collaborate with different clients, and build a strong portfolio. They can also leverage digital platforms to connect with global clients and expand their reach.

Web and App Development

As the demand for websites and mobile applications continues to rise, web and app developers play a crucial role in the gig economy. These professionals can take on freelance projects, developing custom websites, e-commerce platforms, or mobile apps for businesses and individuals. The gig nature of this work allows developers to work on different projects with varying complexities, enhancing their skills and knowledge. They can also choose projects that align with their interests and specialize in specific programming languages or frameworks.

Online Teaching and Tutoring

The gig economy has opened up avenues for remote teaching and tutoring opportunities. Educators can offer their expertise in various subjects, languages, or skills through online platforms. They can conduct one-on-one sessions or teach larger groups, reaching students from around the world. Online teaching provides flexibility in terms of scheduling and location, enabling educators to balance work with other commitments. Additionally, it allows them to diversify their teaching methods and interact with students from diverse backgrounds.

Digital Marketing and Social Media Management

With the increasing reliance on digital platforms for marketing, businesses are seeking digital marketing specialists and social media managers to enhance their online presence. Gig workers in this field can help companies develop effective marketing strategies, manage social media accounts, create engaging content, and analyze campaign performance. The gig economy provides the opportunity to work with multiple clients, gain exposure to different industries, and stay updated with the latest marketing trends and tools.

Benefits of Gig Work in the Gig Economy

Flexibility

Gig work allows individuals to have control over their schedules, choose their projects, and work from anywhere. This flexibility enables them to strike a work-life balance, pursue personal interests, and accommodate other commitments.

Diverse Opportunities

The gig economy offers a wide range of job opportunities across industries and skill sets. Individuals can explore different projects, work with diverse clients, and gain expertise in various areas.

Skill Development

Gig workers often engage in projects that challenge and expand their skills. The exposure to different projects and clients helps them acquire new knowledge, improve their capabilities, and adapt to changing market demands.

Autonomy

Gig workers have the freedom to make decisions related to their work. They can choose the projects they want to work on, negotiate terms and rates, and build their professional brand.

Potential Earning Potential

Depending on the demand for their skills and the quality of their work, gig workers have the potential to earn a competitive income. They can leverage their expertise, reputation, and client relationships to increase their earning potential.

The gig economy offers individuals the opportunity to harness the potential of AI while avoiding job loss. By embracing these emerging job types, individuals can leverage their skills and expertise to work on exciting projects, collaborate with diverse clients, and contribute to the ever-evolving AI landscape. Moreover, the flexibility and autonomy that come with freelancing enable individuals to shape their own careers, explore different industries, and continuously learn and adapt to technological advancements. The gig economy, combined with the power of AI, opens up new horizons for individuals to thrive and remain relevant in the modern automated workplace.

Adapting to Remote Work

In today's rapidly evolving work landscape, remote work has emerged as a game-changer, offering individuals a pathway to stay relevant in their niche or work field despite the advent of AI and automation. Remote work allows individuals to perform their tasks and contribute to their organizations from anywhere, providing numerous opportunities to leverage technology and maintain their professional relevance. By embracing remote work, individuals can explore various job roles that align with their skills and interests, adapt to changing market dynamics, and unlock a range of benefits that foster growth and sustainability.

One of the key advantages of remote work is the flexibility it offers. Individuals can choose from a wide array of remote job options that span across industries and roles. Some popular remote work options include:

Remote Software Development

Software developers can work remotely on coding, programming, and software engineering projects. They can collaborate with teams globally, contributing to the development of innovative software solutions.

Remote Digital Marketing

Digital marketers can remotely manage social media campaigns, SEO optimization, content creation, and email marketing. They can utilize AI-powered tools to enhance marketing strategies and reach a broader audience.

Remote Content Creation

Writers, bloggers, and content creators can work remotely to produce engaging and informative content. They can leverage AI tools for content research, editing, and optimization, ensuring their work remains relevant and appealing.

Remote Consulting

Professionals in various fields, such as finance, HR, or strategy, can offer remote consulting services to clients. They can provide expert advice, analysis, and guidance, utilizing AI-powered tools to enhance their insights and recommendations.

Remote Design and Creative

Graphic designers, UI/UX designers, and artists can work remotely on designing visually appealing and user-friendly interfaces, branding materials, and creative assets. They can use AI-based design tools to streamline their workflows and create impactful visual content.

The benefits of remote work are extensive and contribute to staying relevant in the face of AI and automation:

Access to Global Opportunities

Remote work eliminates geographical constraints, enabling individuals to tap into a global talent pool and work with diverse teams. This exposure to different markets and perspectives enhances their skills and broadens their understanding of industry trends.

Enhanced Productivity and Focus

Remote work allows individuals to create a work environment that suits their preferences, leading to increased productivity and focus. They can utilize AI-powered productivity tools and time management techniques to optimize their workflow and accomplish tasks efficiently.

Lifelong Learning and Skill Development

Remote work encourages continuous learning and skill development. Individuals can engage in online courses, webinars, and industry-specific forums to stay updated with the latest advancements in their fields, including AI applications and trends.

Embracing Automation as an Ally:

Remote workers can leverage AI and automation to their advantage. By embracing AI-powered tools and technologies, they can automate repetitive tasks, streamline processes, and allocate more time for strategic thinking, problem-solving, and creative work.

Adaptability to Changing Demands

Remote work fosters adaptability, an essential skill in the face of AI and automation. As job roles evolve, individuals can easily transition to new responsibilities, acquire new skills, and stay relevant in the ever-changing work landscape.

Improved Work-Life Balance

Remote work provides individuals with the opportunity to achieve a better work-life balance. They can customize their schedules, eliminate commuting time, and allocate more time to personal pursuits, resulting in increased job satisfaction and overall well-being.

Cost Savings and Reduced Environmental Impact

Remote work often leads to cost savings for individuals, as they can avoid expenses related to commuting, office attire, and dining out. Additionally, remote work contributes to a reduced carbon footprint by minimizing travel and energy consumption associated with traditional office settings.

By embracing remote work, individuals can proactively position themselves for success in the age of AI and automation. They can stay relevant in their niche or work field by leveraging technology, accessing global opportunities, enhancing their skills, and adapting to changing demands. The flexibility and autonomy offered by remote work empower individuals to create fulfilling careers that align with their professional aspirations while maintaining a competitive edge in an increasingly AI-driven workplace.

"You do remote work, why are you not a millionaire yet" Martin was teasing me, but I didn't fret. He is quite predictable and I am not shocked by the question. "Everything takes time and consistency. And Coz, you owe me for gas for two weeks. Pay up."